GW00643750

Triumph TR6 Restoration

Published by
KELSEY PUBLISHING LTD

Distributed in North America
by Motorbooks International
Osceloa WI54020 USA.

Printed in Singapore by
Stamford Press Pte Ltd,
209 Kallang Bahru, Singapore 339344, for
Kelsey Publishing Ltd, Kelsey House,
High Street, Beckenham, Kent BR3 1AN
on licence from EMAP National
Publications Ltd
1st reprint 1995
2nd reprint 1997

Acknowledgements

Our thanks to SW Classics of Totnes in Devon who
undertook the restoration, Machine Mart the
sponsors who also supplied many of the tools and
equipment, Autotrim of the Fitham Moor Industrial
Estate, Ivybridge, Devon who returned the TR6,
Abbot Blasting of Newton Abbot and the following
companies who supplied parts: Clive Manvers of
Bury St Edmunds, Revington TR Spares of
Bridgwater, Rimmer Bros of Bracefield Heath
(Lincoln), TR Bitz of Warrington and TRGB of
Huntingdon.
Our thanks also to John Williams for his coverage of
the TR6 restoration project (both written and
photographic) and Tony Hamlin for his coverage in
the TR6 supplement.

ISBN 1 873098 27 8

Introduction

This book is based entirely on reprinted colour articles from the *Practical Classics* TR6 restoration series and the TR6 supplement. It represents the most detailed in-depth coverage of a TR6 restoration ever published. To ensure the best possible quality the whole book has been printed from the film and colour separations used in printing of the original *Practical Classics* magazines.

When I was asked to organise the sponsorship of the TR6 project, Machine Mart seemed the natural answer (having just completed the successful Triumph Vitesse restoration with Machine Mart's sponsorship). Indeed Machine Mart proved to be an excellent choice – they were very supportive throughout the whole series, particularly with their supply of tools and equipment.

The TR6 was considered by many enthusiasts to be the last in the line of true TRs (die-hard enthusiasts dis-count the TR7 as a BL afterthought) and as such was the most modern and useable. Today it is the most popular in the series and the most enduring, both in Britain and the USA.

John Williams is now a veteran of restoration project coverage and his writing and photographs during this series combine to give a lucid, detailed account of a restoration which will no doubt prove invaluable to enthusiasts for many years to come.

Gordon Wright

All prices and company details were correct only at the time that the original articles were written.

Contents

Practical Classics, May 1989

Triumph TR6
SPECIAL SUPPLEMENT
HISTORY • BUYING
RESTORING • OWNING

History and character

The appeal of a two-seater, soft-top sports car is obvious and has remained the same for decades. Nevertheless, Triumph's TR6 differs from many 'sports' models in that it possesses real power and gives performance which remains impressive today, some 20 years after the model was introduced…

To see how the TR6 became a reality, it is useful to look at the way in which the TR models evolved – each version was a variation on the earlier theme, with improvements being incorporated gradually through the years.

The TR story began with a prototype in 1952 which was developed and emerged, in production form, in 1953, as the two-seater TR2 sports car. This was a genuine 100mph-plus machine and was powered by a twin carburettor version of the 1991cc Standard Vanguard engine. At a time when the Triumph name was associated with family saloons such as the Mayflower and the luxurious, if staid, Renown, the arrival of the deliberately sporty TR2 represented an exciting development.

The TR3 was evolved from the original

A product of the sixties still giving exhilarating performance in the 1980s. Tony Hamlin looks closely at this sought-after sports car.

design, featuring a revised grille and more power. The car continued in production until 1961, with changes made to the brakes, cylinder head and transmission, plus minor styling modifications.

In 1961 the TR4 was introduced with restyled bodywork (by Michelotti) and a 100bhp, 2138cc, four-cylinder engine (still Vanguard-derived) now connected to an all-synchromesh gearbox. Steering by now was of the more direct rack and pinion variety, rather than by means of the steering box system previously used.

A derivative of the TR4 – designated the TR4A – followed in 1965. The new car had all-independent rear suspension which transformed the handling, plus a revised chassis frame, although it looked virtually identical to the TR4.

The TR5 arrived in October, 1967, with what was, essentially, TR4 bodywork, fitted to the independently sprung TR4A chassis. However, the new model now featured Triumph's six-cylinder, 2½-litre (Triumph 2000/Vitesse/GT6 type) engine, with Lucas fuel injection. This was quite a departure, for all previous TRs, from 1953, had used carburettored variations of the reliable Standard Vanguard wet liner four-cylinder engine.

The TR5 was, in fact, an historic vehicle since it was the first British (volume) production car to feature fuel injection. At the time only a few foreign makes (such as Lancia) were employing this 'new technology'. The power output, at 150bhp, was impressive and gave the cars excellent performance – a top speed of around 120mph and a zero to 60mph acceleration time of less than nine seconds.

The TR5 was Triumph's first 120mph car but, although much respected, only 1,161 were sold in Britain.

In North America the TR5 appeared as the TR250, with an emission-controlled, carburettored version of the engine giving a less exciting 104bhp.

A 1971, 150bhp TR6 meets a 1975, 125bhp example. Cars from 1973 onwards were externally very similar to the earlier models but featured a 'lip' airdam below the front bumper as well as chrome grille beading, restyled instruments and a smaller steering wheel among other minor modifications.

The sleek styling of the TR6 did not substantially alter during the car's production run. The unbroken line from bonnet to tail helps the car to assume a ground-hugging appearance.

Enter the TR6

The TR6 was introduced in January, 1969, using similar chassis and running gear components to those used in the TR5. However, the bodywork, while retaining some elements of the TR5 design, was externally restyled by Karmann. Apart from smoothing the lines of the car, the design changes also gave it more boot space. A front anti-roll bar now formed part of the specification and wider wheels were also fitted making the car look low, lean and very fast – which, of course, it was, courtesy of the TR5's fuel-injected 2498cc engine. From 1973 this unit was de-rated by camshaft alterations and revised fuel injection metering. Although the engine still developed 125bhp, and was intended to be smoother and more flexible,

The powerful six-cylinder engine is a reliable unit, whether in 150bhp or (post-1973) 125bhp form. The underbonnet view of a Triumph TR6 is similar to that of a 2.5-litre saloon, 2-litre Vitesse or GT6.

enthusiasts often crave for the earlier 150bhp version. This gave the TR6 similar performance to that of the TR5, being capable of 120mph, and sprinting to 60mph in under nine seconds. Petrol consumption was in the region of 22-27mpg when touring.

The TR6 was modified in several respects during its production run and the components affected include the gearbox (ratios) and the optional overdrive (type). The trim was also altered and an airdam was fitted below the bumper from 1973.

A useful option on the TR6 was the one-piece detachable steel hardtop which easily converted the car to a neat sports coupé.

The TR6 came to the end of its production road in February, 1975 (July, 1976 for USA specification models). In all, 94,619 TRs were built, of which 86,249 found homes overseas, only 8,370 being sold in the UK.

The car retained the appeal of traditional British sports models but had the additional, exciting element of being faster and more furious than many would-be rivals. This also helps to explain its popularity today.

The facia is neat and uncluttered, an endearing feature of most 1960s Triumphs. The wooden facia gives an air of quality.

The rear end styling of the Karmann bodywork is as neat as that at the front, with flowing lines which incorporate the tail lamp units and rear bumpers.

The luggage compartment is very roomy for that of a two-seater sports car and an improvement on the boot of earlier TRs. The extended body line gives greater capacity.

The TR6 – the ultimate development of the TR line (prior to the advent of the completely different TR7) – is an attractive, fast and very enjoyable two-seater. Its excellent performance, good roadholding and nowadays – contrary to early reports – relative reliability, plus its sheer character, make it a car which should be high on your list if you are considering a sports car.

The two seats are comfortable and there is ample leg room. The trim is functional, rather than fancy.

Triumph TR6
Buying

It is far easier to see the sort of problems which can affect the structure of a TR6 once the bodywork has been stripped and separated from the chassis. So TR specialists Fortescue Garage Ltd of Bournemouth, kindly let me loose among their numerous TR6s, which included examples too far gone for all but the keenest of restorers, plus several cars in the throes of extensive rebuilds. The accompanying photographs illustrate typical 'danger' areas.

While checking for such damage is not so easy when the car you are looking at is complete (and especially if corrosion has been cleverly disguised), close examination of the vehicle should *always* be made. Both the body tub and the chassis must be checked for rust – and for indications of 'cheap and nasty' repairs.

Chassis

When viewing any TR6 which you are seriously proposing to buy, it is vital to make a very close examination of the entire chassis frame – especially the sections at the rear. The best way to do this is to raise the car on ramps, if possible, and to examine all parts of the chassis and underfloor panelling with the aid of a strong light.

Starting at the rear end of the chassis frame, look at the condition of the two extension members, then at the beams surrounding the differential unit, as well as the main girders – just ahead of the rear wheels – which support the trailing suspension arms.

Quite often it will be found that the tubes housing the rear suspension mounting bolts have broken away from the chassis. Similarly, the welded-in nuts, securing the differential assembly to the chassis, often break free giving a 'clunk' as the clutch is released. To correct such damage, the differential needs to be removed from the chassis, so rectification is not just a straightforward welding job.

The twin fore/aft chassis girders should be checked along their entire length and, at the front, the reinforcing bar between the suspension strut and the main frame on each side. The hefty angled beams inboard of the front wheels should be examined for creasing, indicating a front-end collision at some time. These beams are very strong but will kink after even fairly low-speed collisions. Confirmation of accident damage can be obtained by examining the car under the bonnet. In particular, ensure that the wheelarches, inner wings and front panel are all aligned correctly. A poorly fitting bonnet may also indicate misalignment through impact damage although, equally, it could be due to insufficient attention to detail when a previous owner has fitted new front wings and inner panels.

Sills and floor

The sills must be sound, since they form a vital structural link between the two ends of the vehicle. The original Leyland outer sill panels reach forward into the lower rear edges of the front wings and backwards into the bottoms of the rear wings. So, to replace the sills with 'genuine' panels, the front and

Pay particular attention to the structural condition of both chassis and bodywork, for major repairs to either can be complicated and, therefore, very expensive.

Check the rear part of the chassis very carefully. Pay particular attention to the differential mountings which are often found to be in poor condition.

rear wings need to be removed. Since this is obviously a major operation, some owners have fitted 'cover' sills which run the length of each door but which do not properly connect the front and rear sections of the bodywork. In many cases such cover sills are simply used to cover up existing rust and do nothing for the structure of the vehicle.

Cover panels sometimes can be identified by a seam or gap at each end. However, this may be difficult to spot, especially if the area has been treated to a small dose of body filler.

Make a point of checking the inner sills too, and the outer edges of the floor pans where they meet the sills. Normally you will find that inner and outer sills rust away together and so usually it is necessary to replace both at the same time. This is not a job to be tackled lightly and, if you are looking at a TR6 which has extensive rust in the sills, you should either be very confident about your own abilities or be prepared to face the prospect of very expensive professional reconstruction. Replacing the sills is a time-consuming, skilled job and, inevitably, further areas requiring rectification will be found once the wings are removed from the car.

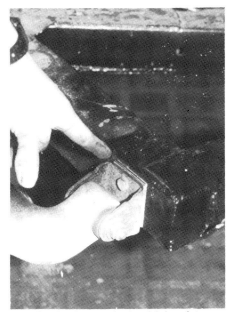

The chassis often rots in the vicinity of the rear suspension arm mountings. Repair is not too difficult provided rust is localised – check the extent of it.

TR6 Specifications

Manufactured: 1969-1975
Numbers sold;
   Home market: 8,370
   Exports: 86,249
No. of cylinders: 6
Compression ratio: 9.5:1
Capacity (cc): 2,498
Max. power (bhp) at rpm: 150 (1973 on, 125) 5,500 (5,000)
Max. torque (lb/ft) at rpm: 158 (146) 3,000 (3,500)
Max. speed (mph): 120 (116)
0-60mph (sec): 8.5 (9.0)
Touring mpg: 22-28
Length: 12ft 11in
Width: 4ft 10in
Height: 4ft 2in
Kerb weight: 2,385lb

The outer sills, inner sills and floor normally rot in unison but check each section individually. Evidence of corrosion as found in the floor/inner sill of this 1971 car means that a great deal of rectification work will be required.

While looking at the inner sills, lift the carpets and check the state of the floor pans and also the horizontal platform behind the seats. Rust is often found here, especially if the hood has been leaking for any length of time. Rust is particularly prevalent in the extreme forward sections of the footwells, adjacent to the inner sills, where the metal receives a bombardment of mud and salt from the front wheels. It is also worth looking closely at the condition of the metalwork surrounding the body to chassis mounting points.

Outer bodywork

TR6 wings are rust-prone and need to be examined carefully although, unless the corrosion has been cleverly disguised, it should be obvious. The leading edges of the rear wings and the trailing edges of the front ones are early candidates for rust perforation from behind, as are the upper extremities of *all* the mudguards. Bubbles in the paintwork are usually the first signs and indicate that the rust is about to break through the panels.

Examine the seam between the bolted panels at the top of each rear wing, as well as the metalwork surrounding the rear lamp units – favourite areas for harbouring corrosion.

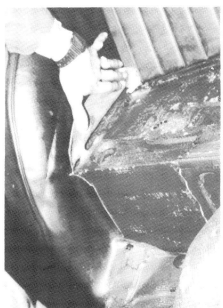

Lift the trim coverings behind the seats for signs of rust. This car was sound here, having recently had new metal welded in. However, many cars will be suffering from rot in these areas.

The rear 'deck' panel, behind the hood, is often rusty. If the seam has parted company with adjacent panelwork, repairs will need to be extensive.

The under-wing areas should be looked at equally carefully. At the front of the car pay close attention to the condition of the anti-splash guards which form a protective barrier between the inner and outer wings behind each front wheel. Once these guards rust away, debris from the road is sprayed up and on to the bulkheads and the forward extension pieces of the sills where they tuck behind the front wings.

From under the bonnet, look at the condition of each inner wing panel from end to end. It is not uncommon to find holes along their upper edges and at their forward ends where these sections join the radiator support panel.

While looking at the bodywork under the bonnet, make a visual inspection of the panelwork surrounding the battery box and the master cylinders for the clutch and brake systems. Spillages of acid and hydraulic fluid often remove the paintwork in these areas and encourage corrosion.

All the wings should be carefully examined. If the rear, lower sections of the front wings have rusted, and the splash guards have disappeared, the chances are that the inner, bulkhead panelwork is also going to be very weak – or non-existent!

On some cars the areas immediately below the bonnet hinges may be found to be rusty and the bonnet itself is sometimes pitted or even holed – normally along the leading edge.

While at the front of the car, take a look below the bumper at the front valance, although these normally survive quite well.

One area which is seldom seen and which can rust away un-noticed, is the rear face of each 'B' post where the front edge of each rear wing bolts to the door pillar. Check the area very carefully, using a bright torch. In particular, ensure that the bolts securing the wing to the door post are sound and clearly visible. If the area has been coated in underbody sealant or filler it is likely to be corroded and has probably been hastily 'repaired'!

Similar checks should be made at the upper and front edges of the rear inner wing panels. Access to these areas is gained by releasing the inner wing trim panels and pulling them clear from inside the boot. While working in the luggage compartment examine the underside of the rear 'deck' and its forward-reaching 'fingers' (behind and each side of the hood); also the depths of the spare wheel well and the lower corners of the boot behind each rear wheelarch where rust is often a problem.

Before departing from the back of the car, make sure that the edges of the boot lid are sound, as should be the inner and outer rear valances too.

Always look closely at the doors on any TR6 you are thinking of buying. Start by ensuring that the outer weather strip, between the top of the door panel and the window glass, is present and that it fits reasona-

bly tightly between the two. If not, water will have entered the door from above and, if this has been allowed to happen over a long period, the lower parts of the door will rust away from within. The areas most susceptible are the bottom edges and corners of each door frame and the outer skin panels.

Evidence of rust damage to the inner wing/bulkhead areas are more easily seen with the front wings removed. With the splashguards rusted through, mud and salt can reach the vulnerable sections of the panelwork further back. Note the drain tube which exits into this area, eventually encouraging rust directly below it.

13

Examine the bottom of each door from below – if rust is found it is obviously a nuisance and a bargaining point. However, bear in mind that it is usually possible to repair the main door frame comparatively easily and that new door skins are available.

Hood and interior trim

Original specification hoods are available for a little over £100, so a car with a rough hood covering can be put to rights comparatively cheaply. However, if the hood frame itself is badly damaged or missing this will cost around £250 to replace.

Virtually all the interior trim panels and carpets are available from the specialist suppliers of Triumph spares, although replacement radio console panels are still difficult to obtain at the moment.

Therefore, while the condition of the hood and interior trim is important, it need not be a disaster if the car you are looking at is otherwise in good condition. Of course, it all depends on the asking price of the vehicle.

Mechanical components

Before considering the condition of the engine fitted to your prospective purchase it is worth checking whether the engine fitted to the car is the correct unit. For early

The inner wings, front and back, need close scrutiny, especially along the panel edges. Again, if rust is severe, prepare yourself for welding in a lot of new metal.

(150bhp) TR6 motors the engine number prefix should be CP, while later (125bhp) power units are designated CR. It is quite possible that you may find a car fitted with an engine from a Triumph 2.5 saloon, producing either 130bhp (early cars) or 115bhp (later models). However, it is also possible to find a TR6 with a saloon 2.5PI engine block installed (prefix MG) but which has been rebuilt and uprated to original TR6 specification, giving 150bhp. To be sure that this is the case, you should ask to see evidence of the engine's rebuild.

The six-cylinder TR engines are renowned for being reliable, long-lasting units, with problems normally occurring because of owner neglect or mis-use, or after very high mileages. So, on all cars (especially if the engine has covered 100,000 miles or more) check the oil pressure at normal running speeds once the motor has fully warmed up. The gauge should show 60psi or more. If the figure indicated is consistently lower, and

especially if accompanied by rumbling, plus oily smoke from the exhaust, an early overhaul will be necessary.

Check, too, for worn crankshaft thrust washers, allowing excessive end-float – this can be felt through the clutch pedal and is definitely undesirable. Again, think in terms of an early rebuild.

Whether such problems will put you off buying the car will depend, of course, on its overall condition in other respects and on the asking price. It is worth considering that the cost of a reconditioned engine – or a full rebuild of your own unit – will cost in the region of £750.

TR6 gearboxes can become noisy after high mileages due to wear in the bearings. The front main bearing is particularly susceptible, as is the layshaft. Another common problem on well-worn units is ineffective synchromesh on second gear.

While the bonnet is open look in the vicinity of the brake master cylinder and around the battery tray. Spillages of brake fluid and acid, respectively, may have led to the disappearance of paintwork and the onset of rust.

Exchange, rebuilt gearboxes are available but the price will be from around £250 upwards depending on the state of the gearbox you are offering for exchange – we are advised by specialist suppliers that on occasions there is very little left to rebuild!

TR6 differentials are durable units, although a whine may set in after a very high mileage.

It is important to check the condition of the lower front suspension trunnions and the upper swivel ball-joints. These components suffer from wear if neglected – conversely, if regularly greased, they will last for a very long time. Look for evidence of recent attention from a grease gun when examining these areas.

On all cars – and especially those to which wider than standard tyres have been fitted – the steering column support bushes and the security of the column itself should be checked. The column can sometimes become detached from its support bracket below the facia.

Normal checks apply to the road springs and shock absorbers; they are still available and are comparatively inexpensive to replace.

Injection – this won't hurt...

When the TR6 was a current production model – and throughout the 1970s – the Lucas fuel injection system was extensively criticised as being unreliable and expensive to maintain. To a certain extent this was due

Lift the boot lid to ensure that the trailing edge doesn't look as bad as this. Sadly this sort of damage appears fairly often on neglected cars.

to a lack of understanding both on the part of owners and others called upon to look after the 'new' technology. However, these days expertise and parts are available at far less cost than in the early days. In any event the Lucas system will provide power and reasonably good fuel economy *provided* that the system is not already worn out and that it is correctly set up.

Another point worth noting is that it rarely makes economic sense to buy a car which has previously been converted to carburettors with the intention of re-fitting it with a fuel injection system. This is because the injection components are normally available only as exchange units.

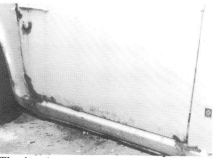

The door bottoms collect water if the window glass sealing strips are damaged or missing. Repairs are possible and fortunately new door skins are available.

Conclusions

Unless you are specifically looking for a TR6 on which to carry out a total rebuild, aim to buy one which is in sound structural condition. It is not a good idea to buy a very rusty car with the intention of carrying out a cheap rebuild. Inevitably, if the work is done properly, restoration will be expensive and time-consuming.

It is also worth remembering that you will probably have to pay quite a lot of money for a car which has been 'glossed up' by bodged repairs and a shiny paint job – you may well end up having to give the car a 'total' restoration to put it to rights, having paid much more than it was worth in the first place. Far better to buy an honestly rough car to start with.

Fortescue Garage Ltd advise that, if buying from a dealer, you should ask to look round the firm's workshop facilities and establish in your own mind that they have the ability and interest to provide any after-sales service that may be required. In addition, make sure that you are given a guarantee with the vehicle. Professionally restored TR6s are not cheap these days and, if investing your money in such a car, you need to know that your investment is, to a certain extent, protected.

Owners' views

Martyn Slater – 1971 (150bhp) TR6

Colin Grierson – numberous TR6s!

Martyn Slater had always wanted a TR6 from the time that they were introduced in 1969. His opportunity came five years ago when his fiancée Jane found a suitable car for him in Manchester, having failed to find one in their home county of Dorset.

The car – a 1971 150bhp model – was in reasonable condition and was used as everyday transport for some time. Its daily duties included commuting to and from work, plus carrying a windsurfing board, strapped to the body sides, at weekends! Martyn shudders now when he recalls the use to which the car was put in those days – the trusty TR6 was also called upon for moving household items such as fridges.

However, when their daughter Charlotte arrived, the strictly two-seater TR6 – by that time the family's second car – was taken off the road. This gave Martyn the chance to strip the vehicle to its bare bones for a full restoration.

By that time the body was exhibiting signs of rust perforation so Martyn worked from the back of the car to the front, removing the wings, a pair at a time, and welding in new metal where necessary to make the structure sound once again. Problem areas included the underside of the rear decking and the inner wing/'A' post sections. Martyn didn't actually need to remove the body from the chassis. Nevertheless, the chassis and underbody were systematically stripped of underbody sealant and rust, then carefully repaired as necessary before meticulously refinishing them – as far as possible to original specifications. A paint-on seam sealing compound was used on all welded joints prior to painting.

Next Martyn purchased a high capacity compressor and spraygun and set about stripping the body shell to bare metal. Having applied etch primer, he refinished the car in red to a truly professional standard. The wheels were shot-blasted, etch primed and then top-coated.

The engine was overhauled, along with the brakes and the rest of the mechanical components. The brake pipes and fuel lines were replaced as a matter of course, and Martyn even re-calibrated the fuel injection equipment before attempting to run the engine. To his surprise and delight it started first time – and ran very sweetly.

The trim was left until last – this has just been completed – so that the car is now in exceptional condition throughout.

Martyn is particularly proud of the fact that the restoration – which took some 600 hours – is all his own work and now plans to tackle another project – possibly a TR4A.

He has kept a detailed record of all aspects of the rebuild on the TR6, with amplification of all trouble spots and methods used to overcome problems – this will be invaluable in the future, both for the TR6 and any other TR which he may tackle. Judging by the superb job he has made of this car the TR4A should also be well worth seeing!

To say that Colin Grierson is a TR6 enthusiast would be a classic understatement for during the past ten years he has owned literally hundreds of them. Today, as a director of Fortescue Garage Ltd in Bournemouth, he is still actively involved with the restoration of the vehicles and his knowledge of the model is second to none. He also still enjoys clocking up miles behind the wheel of a TR6 at every available opportunity.

Colin bought his first TR6 because he felt that the car was a truly practical classic. At the time, the cost of purchasing and owning one was reasonable and he considered the TR6 to be very 'user-friendly'. In particular, he felt that the car, with its solid, reliable engine combined with other mechanical components having no major inherent problems, made life easier for the owner than many high-performance models of the time. In addition, since the basic design of the car was straightforward, Colin found that the TR6 was particularly easy for an owner to maintain at home.

So his first TR6 was acquired, then one car led to another and he was well and truly hooked on the model.

The main virtues of the TR6 – high performance, good looks and ease of ownership – remain although, of course, in the past few years the selling prices of TR6s, like those of many sports cars, have risen dramatically. Colin feels that, this is sadly taking the cars out of the reach of some enthusiasts and his advice to anyone considering buying a TR6 is to do so now before the prices rise still further. However, he also feels that, despite the increasing cost of acquiring a car, they still represent exciting motoring, some 20 years after their introduction. As he points out, with a nought to 60mph acceleration time of just over eight seconds, and a top speed of 120mph (at least for the 150bhp models), the TR6 gives performance equal to – or better than – that of most of today's 'hot hatches', with the added benefit that the two-seater Triumph has 'bags of character'.

With so many TR6s passing through his hands Colin has, of course, gained considerable in-depth knowledge of the cars. He has seen numbers of vehicles which have been allegedly 'restored' but which turn out to be wrecks in disguise. In view of the high prices being commanded by the vehicles these days, he advises would-be owners to take particular care when buying a car. Unless purchasing a budget-priced TR6 with a view to carrying out a total restoration, ensure that the vehicle is at least structurally sound and that the seller has carried out properly any restoration work – a guarantee should be obtained if buying from a firm of professional restorers.

After ten years – so far – of enjoying the TR6, he still admires its blend of looks, pedigree and practicality. "It is", he says, "the last proper British sports car".

Triumph TR6
Restoring

Make a detailed assessment of the state of the car before you start work – and don't remove the body from the chassis unless you have plenty of space and a lot of spare time...

The TR6 is one of the few cars of its time to be produced with a 'proper' chassis frame and a separate body shell. There is no doubt that removal of the body from the chassis will allow better access to the main frame to enable a concours restoration to be carried out.

Equally though, unless you are specifically intending to use the car for show purposes, you should think very carefully about what you will actually gain by separating the units. The job is not as straightforward as might be supposed and, of course, you will need to have a number of helpers on hand when you are ready to lift the body. In addition, you will need plenty of room in which to store the shell and the chassis, once separated, and the restoration is likely to take a considerable time.

If, having taken these factors into account, you still feel that removal of the body is worthwhile, you must ensure that the body shell is substantially sound *before* it is lifted off or it will almost certainly assume a new shape as it is moved!

Therefore, before starting work, it is particularly important to ensure that the inner and outer sills, as well as the main floor pan are strong. If you have any doubts, replace the sills and weld in new metal as necessary before attempting to remove the body. Even then, you will need to brace the body shell between the bulkhead and the tops of the rear wings to maintain its rigidity while it is not attached to the chassis. Convenient bolt holes are already provided which can be utilised for bolting two rigid steel bars in place. These holes are found at the top of the scuttle and at the forward, upper edge of each rear wing (designed for hood frame attachment purposes).

The body shell is attached to the chassis by several sets of bolts which pass through the body floor. From the front of the car, these begin in the engine bay on either side of the radiator and are spaced at intervals throughout the vehicle, the final pair attaching to the tail end of each chassis member.

Sill and wing replacement

As detailed in the 'Buying' section of this supplement, genuine TR6 sills run forwards behind the front wings, and backwards into the bottoms of the rear wings. Therefore, to carry out replacement of a sill, the front and rear wings on the affected side have to be removed from the car. The removal of these panels is not too difficult since all the wings are of the bolt-on variety.

It should be noted that, if you have bought a car with cover sills fitted, it would be worthwhile removing these and fitting the proper, full, BL panels to ensure that the front and rear ends of the bodywork are properly joined before attempting to remove the body! In any event, it is wise to fit new sills while the body is still firmly bolted to its supporting frame in order to ensure the correct relative positions of adjacent panels.

Replacement of the inner and outer sills can be carried out at home provided great care is taken at each stage of the operation and that each side of the car is tackled sepa-

Whether or not you are intending to carry out a 'body off' restoration, the first step is to strengthen the body shell. Luckily new panels, including inner wing sections, can be purchased, making structural repairs a little easier.

Take the greatest of care when aligning replacement panels. Trial-fitting is essential to ensure that the doors, sills and wings eventually will sit in the correct relative positions.

rately (NEVER both together!), to prevent distortion of the body.

Even then, and even if you are not proposing to lift off the bodywork, the structure should be braced between the bases of the screen pillars and the forward, upper sections of the rear wings as already described.

Carefully measure the width of the apertures between each door and its adjacent wing and sill panels and make a note of the readings obtained before you start work. This will give you measurements to work to when fitting the new panels.

When replacing the sills it is important that the front and rear wings and the doors are attached to the car while each new sill is offered up and temporarily clamped in position (using self-grip wrenches or welding clamps) prior to welding. This will help to ensure that the gaps between the doors and adjacent body panels are made as uniform as

possible and that the wings fit snugly. ALWAYS leave the bonnet and boot lid panels in position while the wings are off the vehicle – they give invaluable datum lines to which you can work during re-assembly.

You may not achieve perfection in getting equal gaps between the doors and the wings, for example, but even on an unrestored car you may find unequal gaps and many cars actually left the factory like this. If such variations worry you, steel must be added to panel edges to reduce the visual impact of the problem.

If you work to the aperture measurements made before starting the job, you can at least aim to return the car to its original specification in this respect although, of course, many owners will want to improve matters and achieve uniform gaps!

It is best to take your time during such work to ensure a neat looking finished job.

If you need to replace the sills, or intend to remove the body from the chassis, the body shell must be braced to prevent it from distorting. Two lengths of angle iron, bolted between the 'A' post and the top of the 'B' post at each side, will do the job.

While talking about doors it is worth mentioning that they will survive far longer if the rust-prone inner surfaces are treated to a generous coating of wax-based preservative before the inner trim panels are re-fitted. The wax should be re-applied perhaps once a year for long-term protection.

It makes sense to repair or replace any rotten floor pan sections in conjunction with a sill change but ensure at each stage, by trial-fitting, that all the panels will fit together as they should before welding them in position.

Drain tubes

During the restoration of any TR6, make sure that the drain tubes, fitted at either side of the car below the facia, are intact and that they are not blocked. The tubes carry surplus water from the rear bonnet gutter channel down into the gap between each wing and the inner (bulkhead) panel. If the tubes are blocked or fractured, large quantities of rainwater will enter the car and rot the floor!

Under the original arrangement, with tubes in good condition the water draining through them emerges just above the forward extension section of each sill and eventually encourages rust in this area. A worthwhile modification is to fit longer tubes which will take the water further forwards to exit harmlessly in front of the wing splash guards.

Painting

As with all convertibles, respraying a TR6 is generally far easier than painting any saloon since, of course, there is no roof panel to deal with (unless your TR6 has the optional hardtop). To make the job easier still, and to achieve a better result, it is worth stripping the body shell of all its fittings and trim. Of course, this takes time and all the components need to be carefully labelled and cleaned ready for re-fitting. A TR6 which has all its components tackled in this manner will look stunning once re-assembled.

If the paintwork on your car has had an uncertain past, or if it is obviously suffering from some underlying problem such as 'pinholing', don't hesitate but strip it back to bare metal then start again. Not only will this remove any potential cause of problems for the paint which you intend to apply, but also it will ensure that any areas of filler which have been applied previously to the body-

Once the engine is out of the way, the years of accumulated rust and grime can be seen. By standing where the engine should be, all the nooks and crannies around the compartment can be reached.

work are exposed. They can then be dealt with as necessary – if they conceal rust this can be cut out and new metal let in. Although these operations are, of course, tedious and take some time, they will ensure that the paint finish you apply will be as good as it can possibly be.

Once all the preparation is completed, paint the interior sections of the body shell, then the engine bay and the boot interior. Only then move on to the outer panels.

Even if the body shell is left in place on the

Remove as many as possible of the ancillary components in the engine bay. This clears the way to prepare the panels for painting. Take your time to achieve a top-class finish as on this car, restored at home. The TR6 engine bay has large areas of panelwork which can look superb when carefully sprayed.

When the engine has been rebuilt it can be re-united with the now spotless underbonnet compartment. Great care must be exercised during the fitting-up to avoid damage to the new paintwork.

chassis, all the mechanical units – including the engine and gearbox – can be removed to give access to all the nooks and crannies of the underbonnet area. Take care and the results will be extremely impressive.

Chassis

If you are carrying out a 'body off' restoration the chassis frame will, of course, be very much easier to repair where necessary – especially the upper, horizontal sections which are normally hidden.

Repairs by plating may need to be carried out almost anywhere but one area which is particularly at risk is that supporting the rear suspension trailing arms.

If problems are discovered in the vicinity of the differential mountings (to the chassis) it is worth reinforcing the supports by 'boxing' them in at each side to prevent recurrence of the trouble. As mentioned in the 'Buying' section, the differential has to be removed for rectification work to be carried out on these mountings, so it pays to strengthen them while access is unimpeded. Fortescue Garage make this worthwhile modification to all the TRs which pass through their workshops when undergoing major restorations.

Drivetrain and running gear

The mechanical components on the TR6 are comparatively easy to work on and virtually all parts likely to be needed are readily available. This makes the car an ideal vehicle for DIY mechanical restoration and far better than many other sports cars.

The neat layout allows plenty of room around the major drivetrain units and access to the six-cylinder engine is good.

The overhaul and correct setting-up of the fuel injection system is the one job which is likely to be beyond most enthusiasts and, to achieve optimum power and fuel economy, is best left to specialists who have the necessary testing equipment. However, one check which should be made is to ensure that the boot-mounted fuel pump is correctly fitted on its three 'cotton-reel' type flexible rubber mountings because, if it has been bolted

To make the most of the under-bonnet appearance, the engine needs to be removed. This also, of course, makes it easier to work on the power unit.

All the car's mechanical components are relatively easy to work on – particularly if the body has been removed from the chassis. Brakes, suspension and steering present few problems to the DIY enthusiast.

directly to the bodywork, the vibration of the vehicle can induce air bubbles to form in the fuel, causing erratic running.

In all other respects, the mechanical restoration of a TR6 should be entirely straightforward.

Hood and interior trim

If the hood on your car is tatty, the best advice is to buy a new covering, having first ensured that the main frame is in sound condition. Take great care if fitting the hood material to your existing frame, for the job needs patience and care to avoid damage when stretching the material into position.

If you have any doubts about your ability to fit the material to the frame, our advice would be to seek the help of the specialist supplier from whom you intend to buy the hood material. For example, Cox & Buckles Ltd are able to help customers by assembling the hood for a modest charge. Since the hood is, of course, vital for the looks and weatherproofing of the car, it is worth considering

If the carpets are tatty on your car, new sets are available, to the original pattern. This makes a nice finishing touch to the vehicle after a long restoration.

On completion of the restoration and prior to refitting the door trim panels, it is a good idea to treat the inside of each door with a generous helping of anti-rust wax. This should be repeated annually to keep rust permanently at bay.

having professional help for this job. The thought of spending over £100 for a new hood and then accidentally tearing it yourself during fitting just doesn't bear thinking about!

Clubs and specialists

Owners of TR6s are extremely well catered for when it comes to the supply of parts and services to keep their cars on the road. Indeed, there are very few components which are in short supply at the moment. These include a few chassis sections, front and rear bulkheads, bonnets and front bumpers – these, at over £200 each, are extremely expensive.

It is encouraging to note that when, from time to time, 'original' BL spares become scarce, the specialist suppliers do their best to get the parts re-manufactured – and to a high standard. The situation is being constantly monitored so, in the long-term, all difficult-to-obtain components should be available again.

The club scene is also healthy, with several organisations open to TR6 enthusiasts. It is worth becoming involved with the clubs for many reasons, among the most important being to exchange information about the cars with fellow members and to gain up-to-date news on the spares situation. It is useful, for example, to hear when new lines are being re-manufactured although, as already indicated, the spares situation is very rosy at the moment.

Clubs:

Please enclose sae when writing to any of these clubs:

Club Triumph (Eastern), Mrs. S. Hurrell, 7 Weavers Drive, Glemsford, Suffolk CO10 7SL.
TR Drivers Club, 39 Brook Street, Benson, Oxon. OX5 6LQ. Tel: 0491 35456.
The TR Register, Bill Kendall, 271 High Street, Berkhamsted, Herts. HP4 1AA. Tel: 0442 865906.
Club Triumph Ltd, Malcolm Warren, 13 John Simpson Close, Wolston, Coventry CV8 3HX.
Triumph Drivers Club 1985, Colin Swinbourne, 10 Deerhurst Close, Newbarn, Longfield, Kent DA3 7LL.
Triumph Sporting Owners Club, Keith James, 38 Charlton Avenue, Hyde, Cheshire.

TR6 Specialists:

ACS Classics, Unit 14, Hawkins Lane Industrial Estate, Wharfe Road, Burton-upon-Trent, Staffs. DE14 1PT. Tel: 0283 37120.
Servicing, repairs and restorations.
AM Restoration Services, 1 Firstwood Road, Lathom, Skelmersdale, Lancs. WN8 8UP. Tel: 0695 21849 or 0860 629102.
TRs bought, sold and rebuilt; used spares.
Gary Bates TR GB, 3 Warners Drove Farm, Somersham, Huntingdon, Cambs. PE17 3HW. Tel: 0487 842168.
Body and trim parts, also stainless exhausts and used parts. Cars bought/sold.
Classic Car Restorations and Repairs, Unit 3, Bunas Park, Hollom Down, nr. Lopscombe Corner, (nr. Salisbury), Hants. Tel: 0264 781005.
Top class restorations, especially TRs.
Mike Cooper, West Coker, Somerset. Tel: 093586 2193.
Bodywork restoration on TR sportscars.
Peter Cox TR Sports Car Spares, 89 Fairfax Road, West Heath, Birmingham B31. Tel: 021 477 7966.
Triumphtune parts; major mechanical units.

Cox & Buckles Spares Ltd, 22-28 Manor Road, Richmond, Surrey TW9 1YB. Tel: 01-948 6666.
TR Spares manufacturers and suppliers.
Dee and Gee Auto Repair Centre, 19 Lime Tree Road, Washwood Heath, Birmingham B8 2XG. Tel: 021 327 5211.
TR chassis repairs/straightening; rebuilds and repairs.
East Anglian Sports Cars, London Road, St. Ives, Huntingdon, Cambs. PE17 4EZ. Tel: 0480 67022.
High quality servicing, repairs and restorations.
Enginuity, 236 Trussley Road, Hammersmith, London W6. Tel: 01-741 2387.
Fuel injection work; TRs bought/sold.
Fortescue Garage Ltd, The Old Coach House, Grafton Road, Charminster, Bournemouth, Dorset. Tel: 0202 291691 (daytime) or 888711 (evenings).
TR sales, service, repairs, restorations, new/used parts.
Honeybourne Mouldings, Eclipse Trading Estate, Birmingham Road, Alcester, Warks. B49 5EQ. Tel: 0386 832264.
Body panels and repair sections.
L and M Motors, Rear of 82/86 Southend, Croydon, Surrey. Tel: 01-688 1622.
Servicing, tuning, repairs and restorations.
Marksdanes Classic Cars, A371 Evercreech Junction, Evercreech, nr. Shepton Mallett, Somerset BA4 6NA. Tel: 0749 830862.
TR servicing, repairs, restorations, spares.
Martin's Fuel Injection, Unit 6B, Parsonage Farm Industrial Estate, Stanstead-Mount-Fitchet, Essex. Tel: 0279 816587 (daytime) or 0371 830004 (evenings).
Fuel injection checks/exchange components.
Motor Books, 33 St. Martins Court, London WC2N 4AL. Tel: 01-836 6728 or 3800. Also at 8

Parts prices

These prices, which include VAT but which exclude carriage, were kindly supplied by Cox & Buckles Spares (a Division of Classic British Sportscar Spares Ltd), of Manor Road, Richmond, Surrey TW9 1YB (Tel: 01-948 6666).

Bodywork components: £

Front wing	159.85
Rear wing	159.85
Front valance	156.40
Outer sill	31.05
Inner sill	11.50
Sill end caps (4)	4.60
Floor pan	57.50
Door skin	52.90

Mechanical components:

Engine – short assembly (exchange)	517.50
Cylinder head (exchange)	172.50
Clutch assembly	77.45
Brake disc	17.25
Trunnion bush kit	11.50
Vertical link – left hand	47.72
– right hand	40.25
Steering rack (exchange)	46.00
Shock absorber – front	11.50
– front, Spax adjustable	32.20
Shock absorber – rear	13.22

Trim components:

Carpet set – nylon	86.25
– wool	132.25
Door trim panel	20.70
Boot trim kit	13.80
Boot carpet	14.95
Hood – original BL type	120.75
– 'economy' type	92.0

The Round Way, Headington, Oxford OX7 8DH, and at 302 Holdenhurst Road, Bournemouth, Dorset BH8 8BX.
Wide range of books on TRs.
Northern TR Centre, Sedgefield Industrial Estate, Sedgefield, Cleveland TS21 3EE. Tel: 0740 21447.
Comprehensive range of parts.
M.E. and J.W. Pumford, Unit 4, Corporation Road, Birkenhead, Merseyside L41 8DZ. Tel: 051 653 4313.
TR servicing, repairs and restorations; fuel injection work/parts.
Racetorations, Unit 8, Thornton Street, Gainsborough, Lincolnshire. Tel: 0427 616565/6.
New, improved TR chassis; general and specialist tuning TR components.
Rees Bros., 69 Gordon Road, Aldershot, Hants. GU11 1NG. Tel: 0252 23038.
All aspects of Triumph work, including TRs.
Rimmer Bros., Triumph House, 115 Lincoln Road, Branston, Lincoln LN4 1PX. Tel: 0522 791965.
Body panels and mechanical spares for TR6.
Roadsters, The Old Forge, Crowmarsh Hill, Crowmarsh, Oxford OX10 8EQ. Tel: 0491 38161.
TRs bought/sold, spares, and restorations.
The Roadster Factory, Pennsylvania, USA. Tel: 814 446 4411.
TR parts suppliers.
Sanwa Trading, 1-11-12 Sengoku, Kotoh-Ku, Tokyo 135, Japan. Tel: 81 3 699 5881.
British classic car specialists.
S.M.S. Accessories, 2 Newlands Way, Chessington, Surrey KT9 2RW. Tel: 01-391 1583.
New brake discs for TR5/6.
TR Bitz, High Leigh Filling Station, nr. Knutsford, Cheshire. Tel: 092575 6830 or 6841.
TRs bought/sold/restored; new, used and reconditioned TR spares.
TR Enterprises, Mansfield, Notts. Tel: 0623 793807.
Extractor manifolds, big valve heads, etc.
TR Enterprises (Ron Hall), Haywood Oaks, Blidworth, Notts. Tel: 0623 793807.
Panels, new/used spares, engine work, restoration.
T.R. Improvements, 19 Carnarvon Road, South Woodford, London E18. Tel: 01-505 3017.
New, used and reconditioned spares.
TR Shop Ltd, 16 Chiswick High Road, London W4 1TH. Tel: 01-995 6621/6469.
All spares, mechanical, bodywork and trim items.
TR Workshop Ltd, 3B Quarrybridge Works, Chesterton Lane, Cirencester, Glos. Tel: 0285 69900.
TR spares, servicing, repairs and restorations. Fuel injection specialists.
Triumph Bookshop (Quad Marketing), Welland House, 9 Acorn Close, Lubenham, Leics. LE16 9SP.
Wide range of TR books.
The Triumph Centre, 19c High Street, Botley, nr. Southampton, Hants. Tel: 04892 5683.
New/used spares, repairs and restorations.
Triumphtune, 22-28 Manor Road, Richmond, Surrey. Tel: 01-948 6668.
Special tuning equipment etc. for TRs.
Victoria British Ltd, Box 14991, Lenexa KS 66215. Tel: 800 255 0088.
British sports car specialists.
Yorkshire TR Centre, 50 Thornes Lane, Wakefield, West Yorkshire WF1 5RR. Tel: 0924 365990.
Restoration work, chassis and panel repairs, servicing, etc.

TR6 RESTORATION

Part 1: John Williams introduces our new Triumph project.

We are up and running again with a brand new project starting this month. The car is a Triumph TR6, the restorers are S.W. Classics of Totnes, Devon, and the sponsors of this project are Machine Mart.

If all this sounds a bit familiar, well, you are quite right of course. It is the same team which restored the *Practical Classics* Triumph Vitesse and it is the first time ever that the same restorers *and* sponsors have been invited to tackle two consecutive restorations for this magazine.

Many months ago, during the restoration of the Vitesse, Stan Walters (of S.W. Classics) showed me his own recently restored

Add a bootlid, doors, and outer rear wings (all rotten) and a bonnet, windscreen frame and driver's seat and you have a picture of what we started with. The important thing is that the bulkheads and chassis are repairable.

Most of the front panel is missing and I am not showing you the engine because it is the wrong one!

Behind the rear wheelarches the only panel that we saved in the end was the inner upper rear panel. Better to put £2,000 worth of new panels on a car like this than on one which cost £2,000-£3,000 more in the first place.

TR6. It was, and is, magnificent and a superb testimony to the standard of work that SW Classics turn out. I knew that the Editors were planning a TR6 as their next project car, which was interesting, especially as

What's left of the interior furnishings can be salvaged but the floors are liberally peppered with rust holes.

The nearside front bonnet hinge assembly: One of the two securing bolts extends beyond the captive nut in the inner wing and is used to secure the strap for the outer wing.

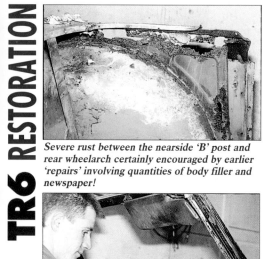

Severe rust between the nearside 'B' post and rear wheelarch certainly encouraged by earlier 'repairs' involving quantities of body filler and newspaper!

Andy removing the instrument panel before tackling the windscreen frame mountings.

The Machine Mart equipment, which includes the space heater (left), a 2ft sheet metal folder and a large parts washer (right) which came complete with legs and all nuts and bolts and was easily assembled.

Here one of the windscreen frame locking screws is being undone.

This shows the offside windscreen frame mounting arrangement with the frame lifted partly out of its supporting bracket...

...and this is the bracket itself after removal.

SW Classics had an unrestored TR6 that was available if we wanted it....

To cut a long story short, we did decide to use SW Classics again, and Machine Mart were invited to sponsor this project which, I'm pleased to say, they agreed to do. If I compiled a list of the companies which started, survived and thrived in the 1980s, when the classic car scene was expanding so rapidly, I am sure many of them would have fascinating stories to tell. Machine Mart are no exception. The founder and managing director, Mike Irwin, started the business in 1981 by selling compressors from the garage of his home in Cheshire. He was assisted by a friend (who is now the general manager of Machine Mart) and by his father, who delivered the goods for him. Rumour has it that Mike spotted the commercial opportunity while restoring his own MkII Jaguar. Certainly the larger items of equipment which we take for granted in the DIY workshop today were nothing like as readily available to amateurs ten years ago. It wasn't long before the first shop was opened in Altrincham and in barely ten years the company have expanded to the extent that they have over 120 employees and 21 branches and two new branches are expected to open within days of this article being published. Machine Mart's 68-page full colour catalogue illustrates a great variety of tools and equipment extending way beyond those required for automotive applications.

Mike Irwin knows what his customers want and he doesn't waste resources on filling his shops with goods which are going to gather dust. Good judgement, plus considerable energy and commitment, brought Machine Mart to their current prominent position and those qualities were very much in evidence during our Vitesse restoration. We have a new selection of equipment to try out on our TR6. Equally important, however, is the fact that Nic Keeley, a senior manager at Machine Mart, will continue to visit

S.W.'s workshop frequently while the TR6 is undergoing surgery. The interchange of information between the restorers and the retailers regarding the capabilities of the equipment, and the popularity (or otherwise) of various items in the DIY restoration market, will enable me to bring a wider perspective to my comments about workshop equipment in this series.

The equipment which Machine Mart have supplied for this project includes a Clarke-weld 120E Mk2 120amp MIG welder, a CSW11 semi-automatic spot welder, a Clarke Plasma King 25 (plasma cutter), an Airmaster Tiger 10/60 compressor, a Desoutter Slimline air drill Model 106, a P5411K angle grinder from the Black & Decker Professional range, a Clarke CW1 parts washer and an Easi-Heat 145 propane-fired space heater. All will be put to good use and I will tell you how well, or otherwise, they perform.

It is easy to spend too much money when buying a TR6 for restoration. Should you spend £1,000 on an absolute wreck or should you invest £3,000-£4,000 on a car which looks better and which might even run? Well, difficult though it may be to remain convinced of this at the time of purchase, the wreck is quite likely to be the better bet. Though the other car may look relatively good superficially, the chances are that when it is reduced to the pile of parts which do not need replacing, that pile will be no larger than the one which came from

the wreck yet you will have spent £2,000-£3,000 more on the initial purchase. The important thing is to buy a car with a reasonably good chassis and bulkhead.

Our car, a 150bhp model, was an absolute wreck. Indeed a picture of it was published on page 52 of our May 1989 issue and I wonder whether the writer was referring to this car when he wrote about examples which were "too far gone for all but the keenest of restorers". It was incomplete and it came with the later engine, though we have a correct engine for restoration. It would be hard to imagine a more extensively rusted bodyshell but, fortunately, the bulkhead was not as bad as it might have been. There is a lot of rust in the centre and rear of the chassis but the front is in much better condition. The chassis and the re-usable panels were sent away to be sand-blasted and it will be interesting to see the extent of the chassis damage and how it will be restored.

The rear half of the body was removed from the chassis in one piece for further dismantling. We saved parts of the 'B' posts.

Parts of the wiring loom had been chopped about to some extent over the years and, if its restoration is likely to take more than one day, it will not be worthwhile but better instead to buy a new loom. Before removing the steering wheel complete with the upper column we cut a branch of the wiring loom which connected to a series of spade terminals on the column. If necessary we could rejoin this later using bullet connectors. While Andy Jackson was busy removing the dashboard and windscreen frame, Stan Walters set about removing the Lucas fuel injector pump from the nearside wheelarch in the boot and the six mounting bolts for the fuel tank. The latter is located under the rear deck panel and the bolts are accessible through the boot.

We cut through the top rail of the front panel, which was all that was left of it, then started removing ancillaries from the engine compartment, feeding the wiring loom back through the bulkhead carefully in case we wanted to keep it.

The rusty outer rear wings were unbolted and scrapped and, when we came to the front wings, the offside one was repairable while its opposite number was so rotten that only the top three bolts nearest to the windscreen stood any chance at all of holding it in place. Each wing should be secured by three bolts down the inside the 'A' post, a row of bolts along the top of the wing, a further bolt through a strap behind the headlamp aperture and more bolts underneath holding it to the sill. Still more bolts should attach the wing to the lower part of the front panel. Most of the front panel was missing on our car.

Before attempting to remove the main bodyshell from the chassis we had to tackle some pretty stubborn body mounting bolts. Why is it that when large areas of a bodyshell have rusted so badly that floors are extensively holed, the strongest parts of it seem to be those in the vicinity of body mountings in which bolts have rusted solid? The body mountings on the TR6 include one on each side at the front of the inner wings, one on each side adjacent to the inner arches, one on each side of the bell housing area in the footwells, one just inboard of

We started dismantling by removing the interior, which amounted to the driver's seat, both seat runners and a few remnants of soft trim. Then we removed the doors, bootlid (which was loose anyway) and bonnet, scrapping the bootlid because it had rusted badly along its lower rear edge, noting that the bottoms of the doors had all but disintegrated and that there was a lot of rust in the upper regions of the door skins too.

Above: Here Stan is working on the body mounting bolts inboard of the rear arches while Andy applies heat with the gas torch, a technique which was needed frequently.

Right: Cutting the floor with the Clarke Plasma King 25. The plasma had to cope with a lot of rust and, though it was a bit hesitant, it did the job which is what mattered.

27

each 'A' post through the floor (four bolts), another inboard and forward of each 'B' post (three bolts), one on each side just inboard of the inner rear wings and, one on the rear of the chassis on each side which is actually underneath the side of the boot. Seatbelt mountings adjacent to the transmission tunnel fasten the body to the chassis as do seat frame bolts and the mounting for the spare wheel.

Before removing the main bodyshell from the chassis we cut it across the centre, between the door apertures. For this we used the Clarke plasma cutter. Later, the two halves of the bodyshell were cut down still further, leaving only those sections which could be re-used.

When dismantling in this way you have to be careful not to throw away brackets, bracing pieces etc. which might be attached to scrap panels but which do not come with new panels such as under the rear deck panel for example. As dismantling progressed, anything which would be re-used was put in cardboard cartons for safe keeping. A little bit of organisation in this way will save time and temper later and, meanwhile, the parts can be stored tidily.

The operation of the plasma cutter is simple in theory and much easier than welding in practice. Very little experience is needed to acquire a good technique and reasonable accuracy. The idea is to press the trigger on the gun then press the tip of the cutter gently against the metal where you want to start cutting and then maintain the 'arc' by holding the tip slightly off the metal (perhaps 1/8in) as you proceed. It sounds easy,

Above: Here the plasma and an air chisel are being used to strip away the unwanted parts of the rear bulkhead.

Left: The panels shown here, all that remained of the original bodywork, will be sand-blasted and repaired then rebuilt in conjunction with new panels.

The companies who have been involved in this TR6 project so far are:

S.W. Classics, Brook House, Dartington, nr Totnes, Devon (Tel: 0803 865842).

Machine Mart Ltd, 211 Lower Parliament Street, Nottingham NG1 1GN (Tel: 0602 587666).

of course, but you should be wearing welding goggles and gauntlets (or one gauntlet, anyway, on the hand which is holding the gun) and these are a bit of a hindrance at first. It is much easier than welding (and a much more neighbour-friendly way to cut metal than with, say, an air chisel) but the Plasma King 25 found it hard going where the metal was rusty or where there was very much body sealant present.

These obstacles are hardly noticed by the

much more powerful plasma cutters which are available for full-time professional use but it is worth remembering that the professionals have to work fast and, usually, they will not bother to clean up metal (with a sanding disc for example) before cutting it. DIY restorers who can afford the time to do this should find the Clarke Plasma King 25 perfectly satisfactory in most situations. It did have one minor disadvantage, however, which was its short tip. A longer tip would

have made the machine easier to use in awkward corners between panels. Stan Walters reckons that the tip on a plasma cutter should be capable of around 40 minutes of cutting which is a lot of cutting before it wears out. It will wear a lot more quickly if it is dragged along the metal rather than held clear of it or if the cutter is badly earthed.

Next month I will describe how we completed the dismantling and we will make a start on the chassis repairs.

TR6

RESTORATION

Part 2: Stripping the chassis and starting repair work. By John Williams.

Our TR6 is one of the 150bhp models which should have the earlier (CP) engine and the A-type overdrive.

This ball joint separator was used to separate the joints between tie rods and track rods.

Having stripped all the bodywork from the chassis, as described last month, our next job was to remove the mechanical parts starting with the engine, followed by the front wheels, hubs, suspension, steering gear, braking components, pipes etc. Then the same at the rear of the chassis.

Everything was heavily rusted and dismantling was hard work. It didn't seem to bother Stan Walters and Andy Jackson however. Mind you, the professionals always seem to have either the right tools for the job or at least a method of solving a problem quickly so that time is not wasted. Also they have the advantage of knowing that if they break anything or create some other problem they will be able to put it right later, unlike most amateur restorers whose skills and facilities are more limited. There were many seized nuts which required heating with the gas flame before they would release and several sheared their bolts but these would have been renewed anyway.

The only problem which occured when removing the engine concerned the brass exhaust flange nuts. There was no chance of these coming undone. Therefore the exhaust manifold was disconnected at the engine and, after removing the engine, the gas wel-

When various nuts are seized and there is insufficient access for cutting tools, the order of operations for dismantling the suspension may have to be varied from that outlined in the text. The important thing to remember is that road spring tension should be kept under control until you are able to release it gradually and safely.

Each driveshaft/hub assembly should be withdrawn while the trailing arm is supported on a jack. Lowering the trailing arm too early would trap the driveshaft.

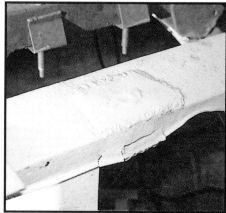

At some stage the front offside diff. mounting pin had started to break through the upper face of the crossmember and an additional piece of sheet steel had been welded over the area by way of a repair.

Then the trailing arm can be lowered sufficiently to release the road spring completely.

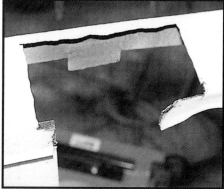

John Holmes started by cutting out the offending area including the bracket beneath and its diff. mounting pin, using the plasma cutter which, you may recall, was the Clarke Plasma King 25 from Machine Mart. Then he used a hammer and dolly to flatten the edges of the metal.

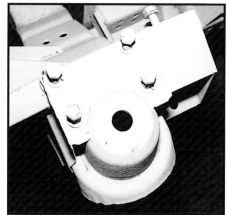

Above: Though our chassis had extensive rust the tops of the front suspension turrets, which are prone to cracking around the welded joints at their perimeters, were undamaged. Front lower wishbone mountings are weak points, too, tending to break away from the chassis.

Right: The new rear axle crossmember assembly. Here the chassis is upside down.

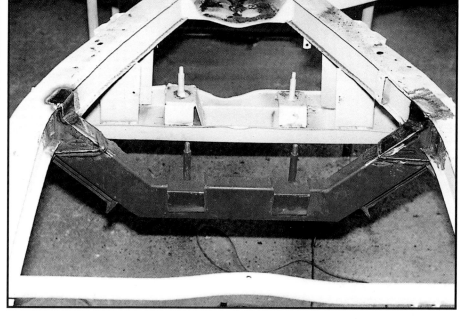

der's flame was used to melt the flange nuts.

When dismantling the front suspension the telescopic damper should be removed first from underneath – it is attached to the bottom spring pan by two little brackets and at its top end there are flats which enable it to be held while the nuts are undone. Then a jack should be placed under the bottom spring pan to support it while the nuts securing it to the lower wishbone are undone. Then the spring pan can be lowered gently

to release the spring's tension completely. After this, the top and bottom wishbones and the fulcrum pin can be removed as an assembly.

The rear dampers, together with the chassis crossmember to which they should have been attached, were missing. The normal procedure would have been to take the rear driveshafts out first then undo the shock absorber link from the rear end of the trailing arm with a jack supporting the trailing arm.

Then lower the trailing arm until the spring drops out.

Note how many shims are found between suspension mounting brackets and chassis, and elsewhere, so that the same number can be replaced in each location during reassembly. This is not necessary in the context of suspension shims when, as in this instance, extensive chassis repairs are anticipated, because the suspension alignment will have to be set up from scratch anyway.

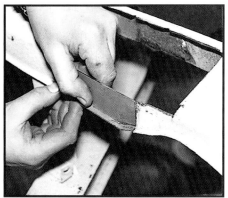

Next he took measurements and, using a small piece of 16 gauge steel (as used on all chassis repairs), made the repair piece including the narrow flange shown here. This was tack-welded in place (Clarkeweld 120E Mk2 MIG), then continuously welded. The welded area was flattened a little with the hammer and dolly (a technique which relieves stresses in the metal as well) then ground down and finally sanded.

Above: After a little trimming the repair section was offered up again and...

... right: tack-welded in place using the MIG welder again. Once more the hammer and dolly were used to flatten the edges which had distorted slightly.

Below: Next the repair was continuously welded (MIG), planished with the hammer and dolly, ground flat and finally sanded so that (apart from the absence of primer) the repair blended into the surrounding metal.

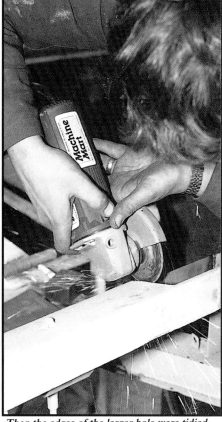

Then the edges of the larger hole were tidied, using the Black & Decker P5411 angle grinder, and the area measured for another repair section.

The repair section was offered up, first when it was a little too wide as shown here. Note the curved forward edge to match the curve of the crossmember.

COMPANIES INVOLVED

S.W. Classics, Brook House, Dartington, Nr Totnes, Devon (Tel: 0803 865842).

Machine Mart Ltd, 211 Lower Parliament Street, Nottingham NG1 1GN (Tel: 0602 587666).

Abbot Blasting of Newton Abbot, Bradley Lane, Newton Abbot (Tel: 0626 68684).

TR Bitz, Lyncastle Way, Barley Castle Trading Estate, Appleton, Warrington, Cheshire WA4 4ST.

Chassis repairs

By my next visit to S.W. Classics the chassis had been sandblasted and given a coat of primer. It was in a rather worse condition than had been suspected earlier, with extensive rust damage in its central area, extending forward almost to the front suspension turret on the nearside. To describe all of the chassis repairs would entail a fair amount of repetition so I will confine myself to a few typical repairs in the hope that readers will be able to apply similar techniques to their own situations. Almost all of the chassis repair sections which we were about to use had been made by, and are available from, S.W. Classics.

In their enthusiasm to get on with the job, our intrepid restorers 'jumped the gun' by fitting a new rear axle crossmember assembly in my absence. However, this is a straightforward job provided that the mea-

All alignments (see text) were checked against all of the other three pins then the bracket and the pin were welded to the crossmember.

Then John 'boxed in' the bracket to give it extra strength – this entailed cutting and trimming two pieces of steel to fit as accurately as possible. This is not an original feature but a worthwhile S.W. Classics modification.

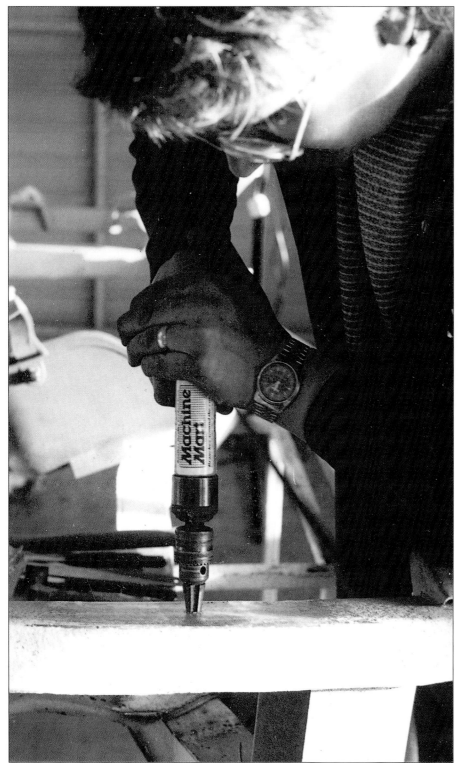

Then the position of the pin was scribed on the metal and centre-punched and a pilot hole was drilled. After this a tapered hole cutter, shown here, was used in the Desoutter air drill Model 106 to enlarge the hole sufficiently for the pin to pass through it.

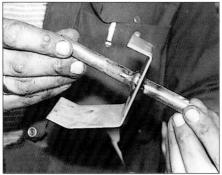

Meanwhile, the pin had been separated from the remains of the old bracket, cleaned with a grinder and fitted to a new bracket made by S.W. Classics.

The new assembly was clamped into place as a single unit, an awkward job requiring careful comparison with the original nearside pin etc. to ensure that the angle of the 'new' pin is correct.

surements given in the workshop manual are applied so that the crossmember is attached correctly to the chassis rails with the correct distances between the fore and aft diff. mounting pins.

Stress cracks in the diff. mounting areas, and broken pins, are not unusual but the crossmember on our chassis, to which the forward diff. mounting pins were attached, had apparently suffered rust damage at some stage and a rather poor repair had been carried out. Though this was not the first job which we tackled, I am starting the chassis repair coverage with this work because it will demonstrate the sequence of operations which applied to almost all of the other chassis repairs. Here I refer you to the pictures and captions.

Just before carrying out any continuous welding (or spot-welding for that matter, though that didn't apply to this particular job), John sanded the edges of the metal clean. The distance between the pins on the forward crossmember was 10½in, centre to centre. When fitting the pin to the new bracket the distance from the bottom face of the bracket to the shoulder of the pin should be 2in.

NEXT MONTH:
More chassis repairs.

TR6 RESTORATION

Part 3: Chassis repairs. By John Williams.

John Holmes grinds the welded areas of the breastplate until it could be broken away from the chassis rails.

There are many topics which will need to be included in this TR6 restoration series so this month I am going to complete most of the chassis repair coverage. To start with I would like to describe, in some detail, the basic sequence of operations associated with welded repairs of the type which we are carrying out again and again on this project. There is little variation in this procedure and I hope that the following will eliminate the need for a great deal of repetition in this and later articles.

The first step is to sand the area clean so that the extent of damage is clearly visible.

Though it is then tempting to cut out all the rusted metal before starting to make repair sections (or to fit ready-made ones) there are three reasons for avoiding this. First, in most instances the amount of metal cut away should be limited to a small area at a time to avoid weakening the structure any more than necessary, then that area should be repaired before moving on to the next. Secondly, usually it will be easier to fabricate and fit a reasonably accurate repair section if the section itself is made ready before the rusted metal is cut away – the repair section can be used as the template for marking the exact area to be cut out. This in itself is an extra reason for limiting the size and complexity of individual repairs and repair sections. Thirdly, some jobs, such as the repair

The Clarkeweld 120E MIG did some good work for us at this stage but if there is one thing which lets most 'DIY' welders down it is those silly little gas bottles which, once part-used, simply do not maintain a satisfactory gas flow. Later on this problem will be eliminated when we will be using the same machine with an adapter (from Machine Mart) and a large bottle.

to the rear end of the chassis which is included this month, call for measurements to be taken before any cutting occurs.

Having made the repair section, and scribed around it to mark the damaged metal which it will replace and which needs to be cut out, you may have a choice of methods of cutting ranging from a hacksaw to a plasma cutter. Whichever method is

The extent of rust damage in the central chassis rails became apparent when the lower breastplate was removed (here the chassis is upside-down). Sandblasting had already revealed lots of perforations in the outer chassis rails on both sides.

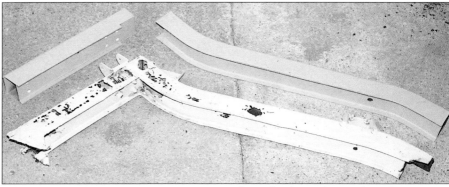

Outer chassis member repair sections, to which we transferred body and suspension mounting brackets.

Repair sections for the central chassis rails were made in accordance with the procedure outlined this month and, while the chassis was adequately supported, rusty metal was cut out and the remaining edges cleaned up ready for welding.

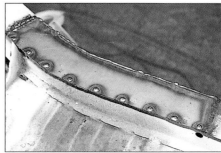

The flange along the inner edge of the central chassis rail was plug-welded while the outer edge was continuously welded (after tacking) with the MIG to another repair section. The welds were then ground and the whole area sanded clean. A new breastplate was welded on later.

used, cut inside the lines which you have made so that the 'hole' will have to be emlarged slightly with the grinder to make the repair section an accurate fit. Allow a generous margin when using a plasma cutter because this otherwise remarkable tool will leave a ragged edge which will need tidying up with a grinder. Next, the hammer and dolly should be used to flatten the edges which will be welded to the repair section (or to reinstate the contours of those edges).

With luck you may now find that the repair section fits exactly into the space which it is supposed to occupy and that it will stay there (even without clamps etc.) long enough for you to secure it with a couple of small tack-welds. If the repair section is a little too small it may be usable still, otherwise make a new section using the old one as a guide though not as an exact pattern of course. If it is too big, clamp it securely to the bench, or put it in a vice, and grind the excess metal away a little bit at a time, trying it for size frequently in between grinding. Sometimes you will see professional re-storers holding small repair sections by hand while lightly grinding such excess metal. Do not do it this way. If the grinding disc 'catches' the metal just for a fraction of a sec-ond it could cause a nasty injury.

When the repair section is ready for fit-ting it should be clamped into place if pos-sible then attached by a few widely spaced tack-welds. Then further tack-welds should be applied at intervals of an inch or so all around the edge to keep the edges together and to minimise distortion during the con-tinuous welding which will follow. You should be ready to interrupt the welding (whether tack or continuous) at frequent intervals to planish with the hammer and dolly. This will aim to eliminate distortion, relieve stresses in the metal and (to a lesser extent during MIG welding than during gas

welding) flatten the welds. Finally, the excess weld can be ground off and the whole area sanded so that the repair becomes invis-ible.

Returning now to the actual chassis work, the first jobs which John Holmes tackled were the replacement of the outer rails at the centre of our chassis, the replacement of one breastplate (using bought-in replacement parts) and the repair of the other breastplate using an S.W. Classics stock repair section.

The first job was to support the chassis, upside-down, and remove the badly rusted lower breastplate by grinding its outer edges, where it was welded to the chassis, and by breaking it away from the very rusted inner flanges of the central chassis rails, using a hammer and chisel where nec-

With the chassis the right way up again John has tack-welded the new outer members into place and is using a straight-edge to check that they are level.

The upper breastplate had rusted along its offside edge only. This edge was cut away, the chassis rail beneath repaired and an S.W. Classics repair section (just tack-welded in this picture) used to complete the repair.

This floor panel may be dusty but it's new and we used it to check the alignment of floor mountings, those on the outer chassis members having been lightly tack-welded into place.

Then the floor mounting brackets were welded continuously to the new chassis repair section.

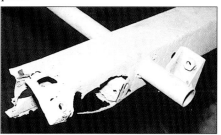

The ragged end of one of our chassis rails needed complete replacement.

The Clarke Plasma King 25 made light work of some of the cutting...

...but the angle grinder was needed to remove the top and bottom faces of the chassis rail from the flanges on the inner face – and, of course, to clean up the edges and the tube afterwards.

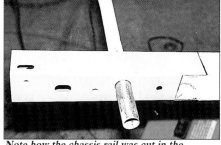

Note how the chassis rail was cut in the previous picture and how this repair section will be welded in for maximum strength.

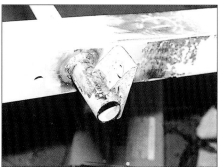

The finished job, ground and sanded and everything aligned correctly.

With the chassis upside-down the dents can be seen in the underside of the crossmember. The affected panel was welded across its full width to the chassis rails at both ends and there were further short runs of weld joining it to the front and rear edges of the box section.

Tack-welding followed by continuous (MIG) welding was the order of the day as usual, except for the flanges which were spot-welded.

essary. This revealed severe rust damage in the central chassis rails and, before this could be repaired fully, it was necessary to remove large sections of the outer chassis rails which were themselves badly rusted anyway.

John tackled one side of the chassis at a time, repairing the underside of the offside central rail, then turning the chassis over to cut away rusted metal along the edge of the upper breastplate and repair the upper surface of the central rail. Then the new offside outer rail sections were fitted (body and rear suspension mounting brackets being salvaged from the old chassis rails) and the S.W. Classics repair section was fitted to complete the upper breastplate. Then we moved on to tackle other chassis repairs and later, in my absence, John fitted new nearside rails and a new lower breastplate.

Where a particular job has to be repeated during a project such as this, for example similar repairs on both sides of a chassis, it is usual for the restorer to do one of those jobs while I am present with cameras and tape recorder and then move on to other things, leaving the remaining job to be done in between my visits. Though I am sure that S.W. Classics could dismantle a TR6 chassis completely and rebuild it perfectly from scratch, I would suggest that to repair one side of a chassis from start to finish prior to tackling the other side – which is what John did, though mainly for my benefit – would be a far safer method for less experienced restorers. By keeping half of the chassis intact for as long as possible it can be used for reference and comparison and for taking measurements. This can be very helpful, even when the workshop manual with all its dimensions and datum points is available also.

When fitting new chassis sections and, later, body and suspension mounting brackets, reasonable accuracy is the name of the game. Particular care is needed in respect of those chassis members which carry the brackets for the rear suspension trailing arms though, even here, there is some scope for later adjustment of the trailing arms by shims between the brackets and the chassis. New chassis members should be fitted level with the rest. Having clamped them into position, a long straight-edge can be laid across the chassis to indicate what adjustment (if any) is needed before welding begins – and it's worth checking this again after tack-welding and before continuous welding of joints is carried out. There is a small margin for error where body mounting brackets are concerned due to the size of the bolt-holes in the floor panels etc. and the fact that these holes can be extended slightly if necessary. Indeed, it is worth offering up the floor panels when fitting mounting brackets to the chassis to ensure that all will align satisfactorily. There is no law which says that all the holes will be in the right places on new panels.

A short section at the rear of the chassis needed replacing and, just to make it more interesting, it was the section through which one end of the transverse tube protruded. As I indicated earlier, this job called for some measurements to be noted because, when fitted, the new chassis section needed to be level with the old (here again a straight-edge

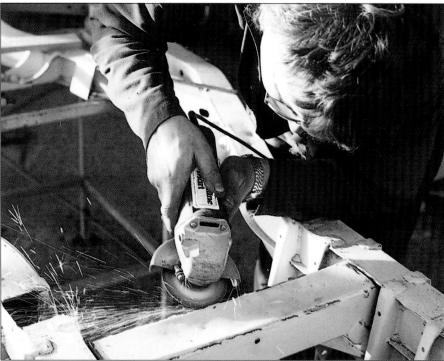

was handy), it had to be the right length overall and it had to be the right distance from its opposite number on the other side of the car. Furthermore, the mounting bracket had to be removed from the end of the tube and this needed replacing reasonably accurately with due attention to the fact that it was not perfectly vertical but slightly angled, like its opposite number.

The tube itself remained *in situ* throughout (attached, of course, to the opposite chassis member) and the rusty chassis member was cut away around it together with the bracket. Note from the pictures how the original chassis rail was cut – and, indeed, how the repair section had to be cut to match. Staggering the cut in this way made a much stronger repair than simply sawing through the whole chassis rail in one place. It made the job slightly more complicated, too, especially as the tube remained in place and the repair section had to slide along it into its position.

The final chassis repair involved replacing the lower face of the forward transverse box section, which must have been used frequently as an unofficial jacking point because it had become thoroughly dented. Mind you, it hadn't rusted and when we opened it up we found out why – it contained a generous amount of engine oil. The pictures and captions tell the story but it is worth mentioning here that the lower face of this box section had two flanges which fitted inside the front and rear faces and the whole thing was long enough to pass under the flanges on the main chassis rails at both ends. Therefore, when the original welds were cut, the dented panel fell into the box section and had to be fished out using a screwdriver. We quickly concluded that to fit the repair section (another S.W. Classics stock item) it would be a good idea to tack-weld a small piece of scrap steel to it, thus creating a temporary handle.

Careful work with the angle grinder followed by the hammer and chisel separated the welds without damaging the rest of the box section, whose edges were then planished.

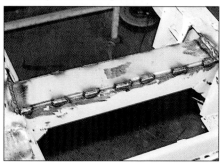

The repair section, which needed to be shortened slightly, was manoeuvred into place using its makeshift handle – here the welding has been completed and the handle removed.

NEXT MONTH:
Restoring the front bulkhead

The companies who have been involved in this TR6 project so far are:
S.W. Classics, Brook House, Dartington, nr Totnes, Devon (Tel: 0803 865842).
Machine Mart Ltd, 211 Lower Parliament Street, Nottingham, NG1 1GN (Tel: 0602 587666).
Abbot Blasting of Newton Abbot, Bradley Lane, Newton Abbot (Tel: 0626 68684).
TR Bitz, Lyncastle Way, Barley Castle Trading Estate, Appleton, Warrington, Cheshire WA4 4ST (Tel: 0925 861861, Fax: 0925 860816).
Rimmer Bros Ltd, Triumph House, 115 Lincoln Road, Branston, Lincoln LN4 1PX (Tel: 0522 791965, Fax: 0522 794118).
The principal clubs which specialise in the Triumph TR range are:
The TR Register, Phil Edwards, 8 Gorse Close, Droitwich, Worcestershire WR9 7SG.
TR Drivers' Club, 39 Brook Street, Benson, Oxon. OX9 6LQ (Tel: 0491 35456).

Fitting the new bulkhead front panels (in effect the front of the footwells) was a straightforward clamping and spot welding job (or plug welding where the spot welder wouldn't reach). These replacement panels are made by S.W. Classics. John should be wearing safety goggles and gauntlets here.

TR6
RESTORATION

Part 4: Front bulkhead repairs. By John Williams.

You may recall that very little of the original TR6 bodyshell was saved after dismantling. Four inner wheelarches, about half of the front bulkhead, the transmission tunnel and a few odds and ends just about sums it up. I was beginning to think that the rebuild would be a massive undertaking, not only on account of the number of replacement panels that would have to be incorporated but also because of the problems that reproduction panels can cause.

The original front wheelarches with parts of the old bulkhead which will be rebuilt using the new panels at front and right of picture.

As usual, S.W. Classics made it look easy. The first job was to repair and rebuild the front bulkhead and front wheelarches and to add some mounting brackets to a pair of new floor panels. Then the rear bulkhead was dismantled and the salvaged components repaired. The doors and windscreen frame needed attention, too, then we were ready for the first 'trial fitting' of the entire body-

shell. The new floor panels were bolted loosely to the chassis and the inner sills were tacked into place. Next the front bulkhead, the transmission tunnel and the old and new components of the rear bulkhead were

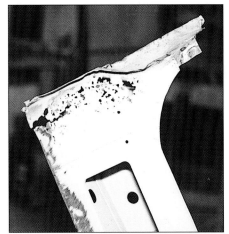

This is typical rust damage as found at the bottom of our nearside 'A' post.

The bracket in the base of each 'A' post was badly rusted too. Here the repair section for the inner face of the 'A' post has been clamped in place and this will be welded along its upper edge only until the bodyshell is rebuilt, when the inner sill will pass between this repair section and the rest of the 'A' post.

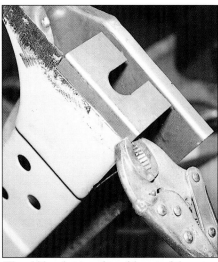

The old bracket together with part of the outer face of the 'A' post was cut out, flattened and used as a pattern to scribe its outline on new sheet steel. A couple of tack welds secured the new bracket while repair work continued.

The next job was to add a new piece to the front face of the 'A' post. Note that, like the repair section for the inner face, this was made too large at first so that it could be trimmed to size. This, too, was tack welded at first, then continuously welded as shown here prior to grinding.

Above the 'A' post the edge of the bulkhead top panel needed replacing and the first job was to measure the area which needed repairing...

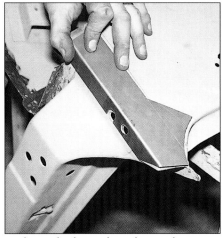

...then make the repair section, as shown here, then scribe around it to mark out the area to be cut out.

clamped into place and it was time to add the outer panels, starting with the front wings. It seemed that in no time we were looking at a TR6 bodyshell again but, in fact, the front bulkhead repairs alone had kept John Holmes busy for two days and John doesn't waste time.

I am jumping ahead a bit here and will be looking more closely at the jobs just outlined during the next couple of months. Through the pictures and captions this month I want to show you some of the work carried out on the front bulkhead which was in a pretty bad way. We needed replacement panels for the fronts and sides of the footwells, the bottoms of the 'A' posts were rotten and there were rust holes in the nearside end of the top panel and in some of the forward-facing panels. Some of the smaller holes in the panels under the bulkhead were brazed as there was no good reason to spend a disproportionate amount of time on them.

Finally, over the years we have repeatedly recommended the use of appropriate safety

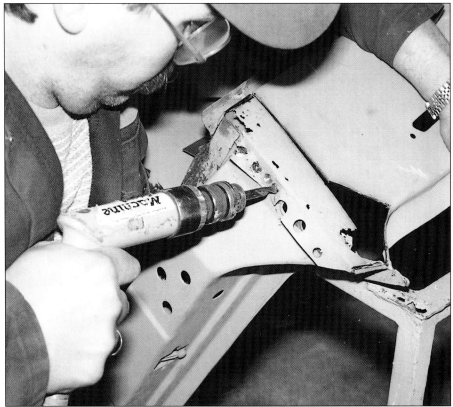

There were spot welds to be broken, which entailed drilling the top layer of metal only, then separating it from the layer beneath using a hammer and cold chisel as necessary.

Fortunately only the outer skin of the bulkhead had rusted.

A small repair section was made for the forward end of the damaged area, tacked into place and the excess metal trimmed off.

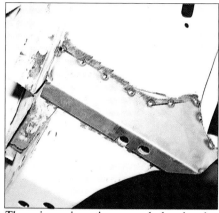

The main repair section was tacked to the edge of the top panel and spot welded along its outer flange, then both repairs were continuously welded around the edges which had been tacked previously.

Finally the whole repair was sanded.

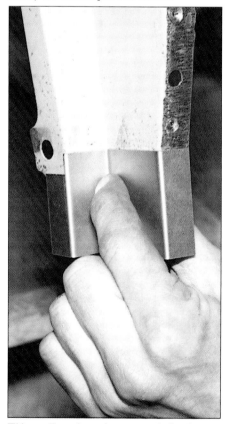

This small repair section was made for the lower nearside part of the bulkhead which lies alongside the transmission tunnel. It was made slightly over length, welded on, then cut to length later to suit requirements.

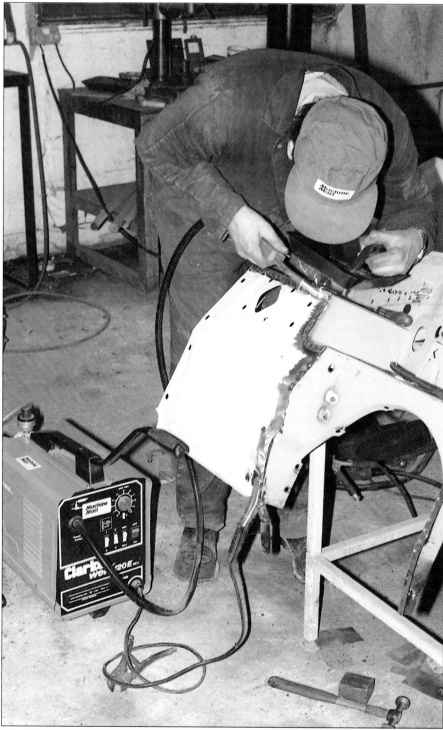

John Holmes using the Clarkeweld 120E to plug weld the inner edge of the new offside front bulkhead panel – an area which the arms of the spot welder were not quite long enough to reach.

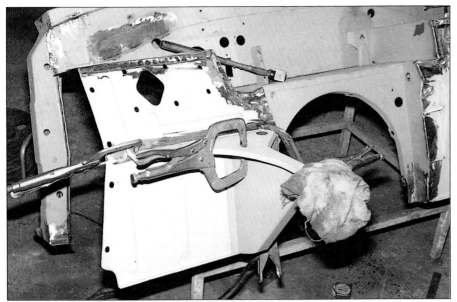

Next the additional panels for the front of the bulkhead were clamped together and then to the bulkhead. Measurements were checked against the original assembly before spot welding started. The front of the panel which follows the contour of the inner wheelarch comes to a very sharp point – hence the piece of rag for safety's sake.

With the bulkhead almost upside-down on the supporting frame the side panel was clamped into place and spot welded. The Clarke CSW11 spot welder from Machine Mart has proved to be a reliable unit.

The offside front bulkhead was completed by the addition of the splash guard, which John is holding in position here and which is secured by four screws into nuts on the outer flange of the bulkhead.

The companies who have been involved in this TR6 project so far are:

S.W. Classics, Brook House, Dartington, nr Totnes, Devon (Tel: 0803 865842).
Machine Mart Ltd, 211 Lower Parliament Street, Nottingham, NG1 1GN (Tel: 0602 587666).
Abbot Blasting, Bradley Lane, Newton Abbot (Tel: 0626 68684).
TR Bitz, Lyncastle Way, Barley Castle Trading Estate, Appleton, Warrington, Cheshire WA4 4ST (Tel: 0925 861861, Fax. 0925 860816).
Rimmer Bros Ltd, Triumph House, 115 Lincoln Road, Branston, Lincoln LN4 1PX (Tel: 0522 791965, Fax. 0522 794118).

The principal clubs which specialise in the Triumph TR range are:

The TR Register, 271 High Street, Berkhampstead, Herts. HP4 1AA.
TR Drivers' Club, 39 Brook Street, Benson, Oxon. OX9 6LQ (Tel: 0491 35456.

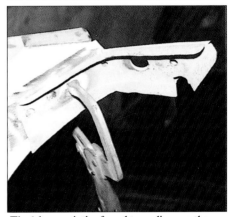

The 'sharp point' referred to earlier was then eliminated by the addition of this stiffening bracket.

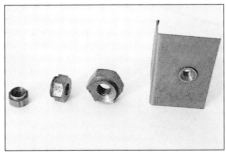

The 'nuts' for the splash guards were actually rivet bushes like these. They are available in several sizes and to suit various thicknesses of metal. For each bush a hole of appropriate size is drilled (or punched) in the metal, the bush is inserted and then peened over rather like a rivet, as shown in the sample here.

equipment in the workshop. However, it is our experience that individual professional restorers exercise a fair amount of discretion regarding the extent to which this recommendation is applied. Therefore when, from time to time, the relevant safety equipment is absent from pictures used in this series it reflects the reality of the situation rather than any change in our policy regarding safety.

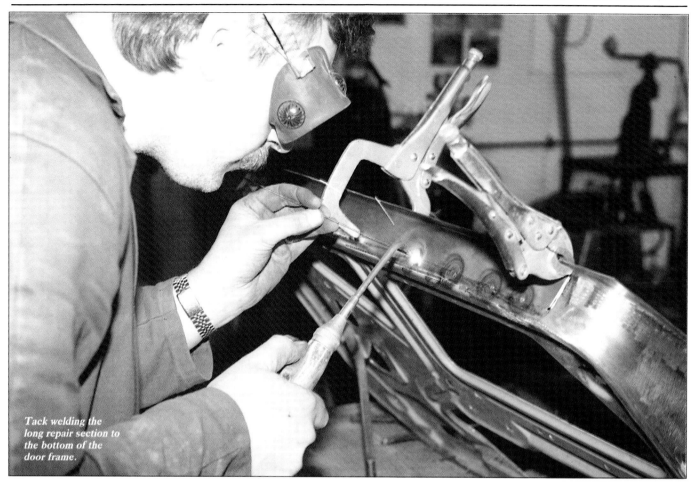

Tack welding the long repair section to the bottom of the door frame.

TR6 RESTORATION

Part 5: Door frame repairs. By John Williams.

If you visited the Bristol Classic Car Show in March you will know that the restoration of our TR6 had moved a long way ahead of the story by that time. The bodyshell was displayed on the chassis at the show and it attracted a lot of interest. SW Classics had put in a great deal of extra time on this project prior to the show to make the car worth displaying. There were one or two spectators who pronounced loudly on this or that supposed fault or other aspect of the work which could have been done better. What they didn't realise (and certainly didn't bother to find out) was that there had been no special preparation and the bodyshell reassembly work had not been finished by any means. I suppose a few unjustified and unkind comments have to be expected at shows – where would show business be without the comedians?

This month, through the pictures and captions, I am going to show you some typical door frame repairs. As usual the equipment which we had borrowed from Machine Mart played its part in the proceedings and this included sanders, grinders, the Clarke CSW11 Spot Welder, the Desoutter Model 106 Air Drill, welding clamps and the 33lb anvil. The latter is the largest of a range of three anvils from Machine Mart and it seems to be the ideal size, being portable but not inclined to move about when in use.

The MIG welder and plasma cutter took a back seat this month, not due to any dissatisfaction with them but simply because we didn't need the plasma and John Holmes reached for the gas torch almost instinctively. When asked why, I was relieved to note that John didn't highlight any shortcomings of the Clarke MIG welder in particular but pointed out that, in general, gas welding has certain advantages over MIG. First, with gas welding you don't get such a build-up of weld because you have much better control over the amount of new metal fed into the weld. Secondly, gas welding makes a softer weld which is easier to planish using the hammer and dolly. Thirdly, though you can regulate the wire speed on a MIG welder this does not necessarily provide sufficient control when working on thin metal where there is a tendency to blow holes in the work. It is worth bearing in mind in this context that, for example, 20

By sanding all around the side and bottom edges of the skin, and along the top front edge, the outer skin, the door frame flange and the inner fold of skin could be separated.

gauge steel is 0.914mm or 0.035in thick. By the time this has been sanded (perhaps on both sides), to remove surface rust and to prepare it for welding, it could be substantially thinner while perfectly adequate still for its job.

Our doors had rusted badly along their bottom edges and around the corners at both ends and there was heavy rust on the inside of the door skins above the swage line. John had removed all door fittings previously and the first job was to remove a skin. The pictures take up the story.

Next month I will describe re-skinning a door, followed by some windscreen frame repairs. □

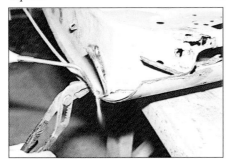

The gas flame was used to melt the brazed areas at the front and rear ends of the swage line, the front end of the window aperture and, at the top rear of the door skin in the corner.

With the skin removed John sanded all around the flange and adjacent areas of the door frame to discover the extent of the damage and the first repair was to the bottom rear corner of the door shown here.

A piece of sheet steel was cut out, oversize at first, then shaped on the anvil and trimmed in small stages to the required size.

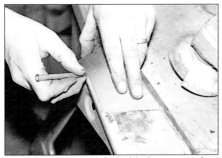

When John was satisfied with the new repair section he scribed around it on the door frame to mark the extent of the old metal to be cut out.

Next, another piece of new steel was held against the door frame while the outline of the door frame flange was scribed on to it.

Then this new piece was cut, tried for size and trimmed as necessary to replace the original flange in the area.

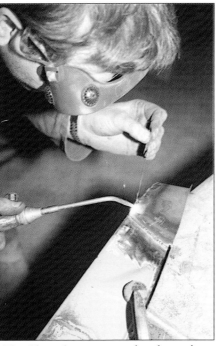

The old metal was cut away then the repair section was trial fitted and tack welded, followed by continuous welding.

A little work with the hammer and dolly was needed while welding the edge of the repair section to the cut edge of the door frame (the lower edge in this picture) to keep the two edges in alignment.

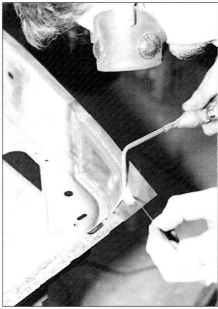

Then the flange repair section was tacked into place and continuously welded in a similar way and then planished to flatten the welds and sanded to make it neat and tidy.

TR6 RESTORATION

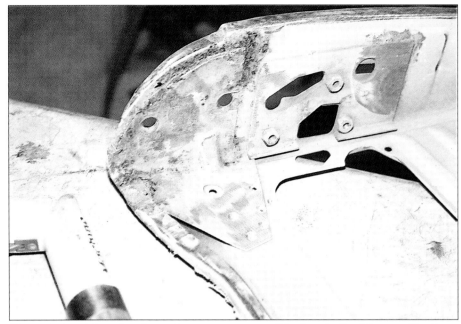

To repair the reinforced section at the upper rear corner of the door the first job was to identify and drill the spot welds and peel the reinforcing piece away using a hammer and chisel. If in reasonable condition this piece could be flattened again and reused but ours was rusty and ragged around the edges.

The next job was to measure the rusted area at the bottom of the door frame and to cut and fold the repair section shown here, whose outline was scribed on to the frame before the old metal was cut out.

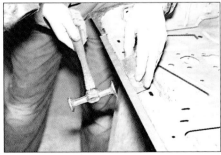

The heading picture shows the tack welding in progress and here John is planishing during welding to keep the adjacent edges flat and straight.

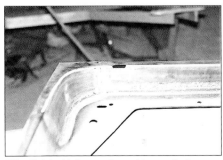

The finished job complete with new drainage slot – made by drilling holes and using a thin round file to join them.

A repair section was cut from sheet steel and trimmed to the exact shape and size required. SW's bench mounted hole punching machine was used to make the two ⅛in holes to match the original.

Next, John made a new flange while the old one was in place still to act as a pattern...

...where it was tack welded then continuously welded

The old reinforcing section was tidied up with the hammer on the 33lb anvil and its outline was marked on a new sheet of steel and then cut out. The positions of the two $\frac{5}{8}$in holes and the slot were marked carefully (as per the original) and the punch was used again.

With the repair section held firmly in place the door was scribed to mark the extent of the metal to be removed and then the old metal was cut away.

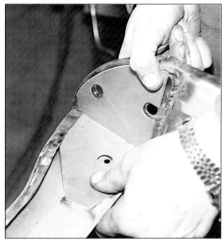

Here John is positioning the new reinforcing section...

...prior to spot welding it into place using the Clarke CSW11 Spot Welder, a tool whose reliability has exceeded the expectations of our professionals.

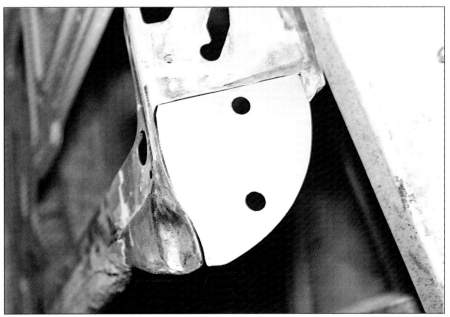

This is the new repair section in position...

The principal clubs which specialise in the Triumph TR range are:

The TR Register, 271 High Street, Berkhamstead, Herts, HP4 1AA.
TR Drivers' Club, 39 Brook Street, Benson, Oxon, OX9 6LQ. Tel. 0491 35456.

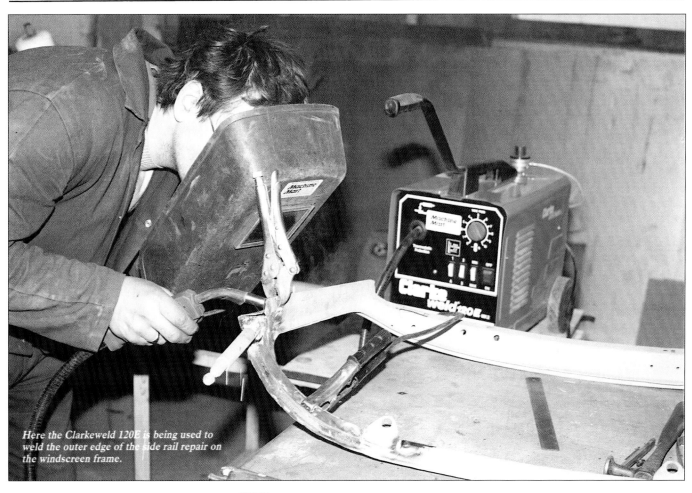

Here the Clarkeweld 120E is being used to weld the outer edge of the side rail repair on the windscreen frame.

TR6 RESTORATION

Part 6: Door skinning and repairs to the 'B' post and windscreen frame. By John Williams.

Though our TR6 windscreen frame required some repairs we thought that we ought to find a better example of typical damage for these articles. As luck would have it S.W. Classics had a frame from a Mk 3 Spitfire (basically the same frame as the TR6 plus rainwater channels) and it is the repairs to this frame which are featured this month.

I am also going to show how we saved money when repairing the 'B' posts (the publishers should be proud of us!) and I am including a few words about re-skinning a door.

On the windscreen frame there were rust holes in the underside and forward flange at both ends of the bottom rail and also in the bottom inch or two of the side rails – hidden in this instance behind equally rusty rainwater channels. The repair section for the front flange was made from two narrow strips of steel. These were cut a little oversize then shaped by the cross pein hammer on the 33lb anvil from Machine Mart – a most useful tool.

When re-skinning each door the first task was to offer up the new skin to make sure that it would fit the frame. This cannot be taken for granted. Then the labels were removed from the skin and a sound deadening pad was fitted to the inner face of the skin – a matter of removing the backing paper from the pad, heating the pad slightly in the warm air from the workshop heater to make it more pliable, then pressing it into place.

Then, with the skin carefully aligned around the frame, its front and rear edges were folded over the frame first, using the hammer and dolly, followed by the top and bottom edges which, being straight rather than curved, could be supported by the bench rather than the dolly. The secret of successful fitting is to turn the whole of each edge a little at a time to avoid distorting the metal. The top rear corner of the skin and frame, where there is hardly any overlap, were secured by a spot of braze. After the skin had been fitted further brazing was done behind the swage line at each end of the door where there are gaps in the flange of the skin and along a couple of inches down the edge of the flange at the top rear of the door (to join up with the small braze which we applied earlier), also where the skin flange comes to an end at both ends of the window aperture and again just forward of the window aperture under the edge of the skin. In effect no bare ends were left on flanges, all were either welded or brazed.

The pictures and captions take up the story.

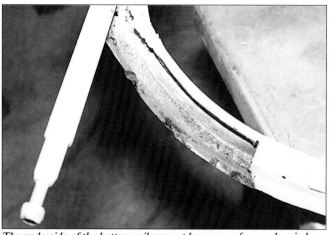

The underside of the bottom rail was cut by means of an angle grinder and remnants of metal along the flange peeled away. The hammer and dolly were used to flatten out the flange. The edges were cleaned up by grinding and sanding.

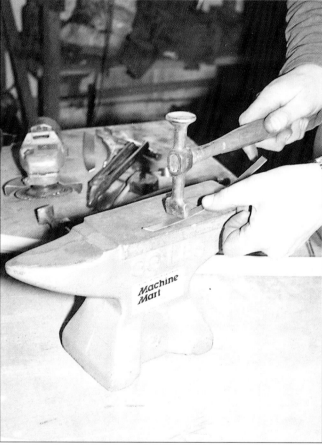

To produce the required curves in the straight strips of steel John Holmes concentrated the hammer blows along one edge, thus stretching the metal.

The two curved strips of steel were then lightly tack-welded...

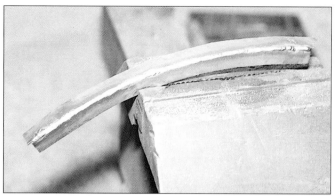

...followed by continuous welding

Then they were clamped in place to be spot-welded to the frame.

Next John had to cut out a piece of new steel and trim it carefully to fill the remaining gap in the underside of the frame...

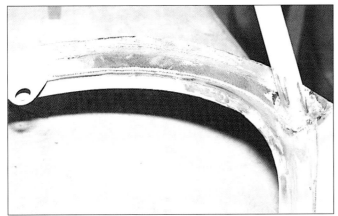

... This too was tacked into place and then continuously welded.

Here the rainwater channel (not present on the TR6) has been removed from the rear face of the side rail by drilling out the spot welds. The outer edge of the rusty area has been cut by disc and the flange separated by hammer and chisel.

Here the small repair section has been trimmed to size. If the whole rear face of the side rail had needed replacing John would have made up a full-length section with an inboard flange and a small outboard flange which could tuck in behind the existing outer edge of the frame. The hole in the repair section enabled John to braze through it on to the windscreen frame support.

This is the finished repair.

The bottom couple of inches of each 'B' post was rusty so John used S.W. Classics repair sections, which determined where the 'B' posts had to be cut.

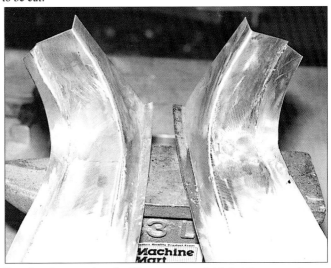

Complete front sections for 'B' posts are available but they are quite complicated panels and therefore expensive. Generally it is only the bottom two to three inches of the 'B' post which rusts.

A finished door frame which has had its bottom edge and flange replaced and repairs to all four corners.

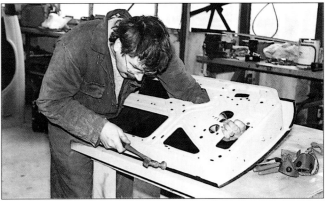

The dolly was not used all the time when re-skinning the door. The important thing is that the door must be supported firmly, by the dolly or the bench, directly under the hammer.

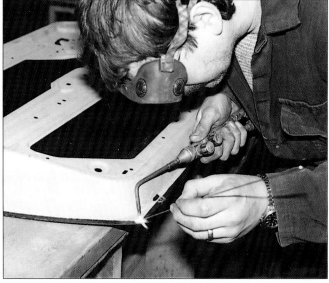

Having fitted the skin John welded behind the top front corner and both bottom corners...

...then brazed all the areas mentioned in the text and applied the finishing touches by sanding lightly around the outer edges of the skin and running a file along the edges.

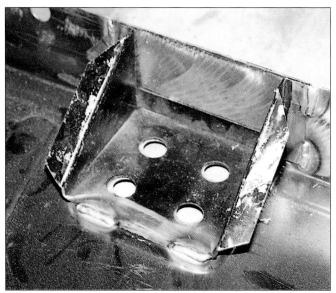

Mounting brackets were welded to the replacement floor panels. The bracket shown here is one of the forward ones and is an original part.

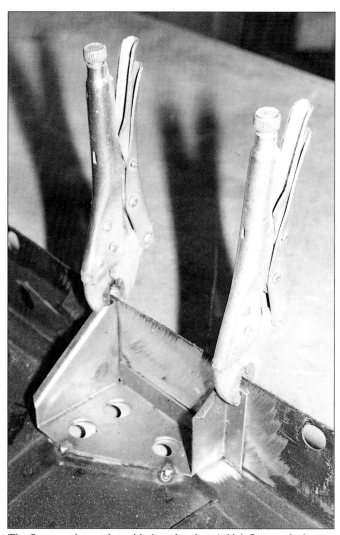

The floor panels together with these brackets (which fit towards the rear of the floor) were remanufactured; the alignment of the bolt holes in the floors could have been better.

The remains of the rear bulkhead prior to being cleaned up ready for rebuilding.

TR6
RESTORATION

TR6 RESTORATION

Part 7: This month, John Williams deals with dismantling and cleaning the engine and finding the faults.

● *The almost indispensable extractor which was used to remove the cylinder head studs.*

By way of a change I am setting aside bodywork restoration this month to look instead at the engine overhaul. We had no way of knowing what we would find as Phil Dickinson started to dismantle the engine but it was reasonable to assume that it had been neglected for some time.

Ours is the 150bhp CP engine. The later 125bhp CR engine differs in subtle ways. For example it has a different camshaft and the fuel injection metering unit is calibrated differently to suit.

The order in which dismantling took place was conventional and we had no real difficulties. The rocker cover came off first followed by the rocker assembly.

The cylinder head was next and this required a bit of persuasion, so a mallet was used to help break the gasket seal. The cylinder head studs were next and then Phil turned his attention to the flywheel, which was secured by four bolts in the crankshaft flange.

The backplate came off next and then the engine was turned upside-down and the sump removed. The damper and pulley

● *If you are overhauling an unfamiliar engine, remember to keep all the nuts, bolts etc. in groups with the components to which they belong, to avoid confusion when reassembling.*

assembly was loosened and removed from the front of the crankshaft by striking its perimeter with a mallet, turning the crankshaft at intervals so that the mallet could be applied all the way around the perimeter.

The timing cover came off next followed by the camshaft timing gear and the duplex chain, then the crankshaft oil seal sleeve and oil deflector followed by the sprocket (behind which shims may be fitted to align the sprocket with the camshaft gear). The crankshaft sprocket (keyed on to the shaft) was a bit stubborn but not as bad as the engine's front plate, which had been well and truly glued by the gasket seal which had been used the last time it had been refitted. Before we could tackle the front plate, however, we removed the horseshoe-shaped camshaft locating plate (two bolts).

Valve removal

The oil seal housing was removed from the rear end of the engine and the sealing block ▶

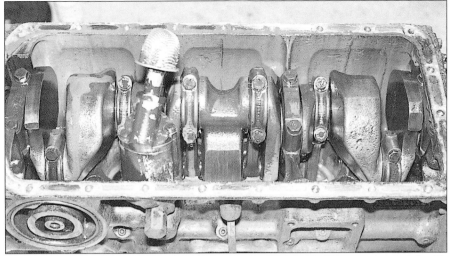

● *The big end bearings proved to be 0.0030in undersize so we plan to fit a new crankshaft for this engine.*

● *The bottom centre bolt through the timing cover should be shorter than the others.*

● *The larger timing gear is attached to the camshaft by two bolts and, with these undone, the gear and chain can be removed easily.*

● *The case-hardening on some of the camshaft lobes was beginning to disintegrate as shown here. A Piper cam will be fitted.*

● *With the securing bolts undone the rear oil seal housing can be removed over the crankshaft flange.*

TR6 RESTORATION

● *Removing the sealing block from the front of the crankcase.*

was removed from the front where, when the engine is upside-down, it covers the front main bearing.

The oil pump was removed by unscrewing the three long bolts which secure it to the crankcase, lifting out the filter and casting in one piece and then the housing and rotors as a separate assembly. On the block all that remained was to undo the big end and main bearing bolts and remove them with bearing caps and shells and, having turned the block on to its side, to withdraw the pistons and conrods.

When removing the valves from the cylinder head, the first step is to strike the top of each valve assembly with a mallet to ease the valve collars and cotters and then it is just a matter of using a suitable valve spring compressor to shorten each set of double springs in turn while the cotters and upper collars are removed. The upper collars on the inlet valves are in one piece. On the exhaust valves they are in two parts and it is worth checking the outer ones for cracks.

Efficient washer

Thanks to the project's sponsors, Machine Mart, S.W. Classics could hardly have been better equipped to clean components as this particularly filthy engine was dismantled. The star turn was the floor—standing version of the Clarke Parts Washer. I must admit that when I heard about this machine I reckoned that it would get a very low priority rating from most DIY restorers who were buying workshop equipment. After all, who would want to pay around £180 (including delivery and the current extortionate rate of VAT) for such a tool or, around £92 for the bench—mounted version?

Well, the answer, now that I have seen the parts washer in action and used it myself, is me. One of the few aspects of overhaul and restoration work which causes me a great deal of grief is the need to clean components efficiently. In the past I have used the "bucket of paraffin and an old paint brush" method, wasting a great deal of the cleaning fluid, and a great deal of time, while trying to apply enough fluid to clean and rinse each component.

The Clarke Parts Washer does a very good job in a much shorter time. The floor—standing model (capacity ten gallons – but it will work quite happily with half that amount) delivers a steady stream of cleaning fluid to where it is needed, leaving the operator free to concentrate on handling the component and using a cleaning brush as necessary.

The cleaning fluid passes from the reservoir within the washer through an electric pump to a flexible spout. Large items for cleaning (up to the size of a TR6 engine block) can be rested on a platform which is above the level of the fluid inside the washer. A separate, removable container with a perforated base is supplied with the washer and this is ideal for holding smaller components while the cleaning fluid drains away.

Safety device

We used DUCO engine degreasant in the parts washer. This has an advantage over thinners, for example, in that it doesn't remove paint.

Many of the cleaning fluids which might be used are inflammable and the Clarke Parts Washer has a cunning built-in safety device which consists of a support for the hinged lid which melts in the event of fire, allowing the lid to drop and smother the fire.

It was great to see all the components shining brightly on sheets of paper on the floor within minutes of being removed from the engine. However, some items, the rocker and timing covers for example, needed washing and then blasting to remove old paint and rust.

Blasting cabinet

This was no problem as we had another of Machine Mart's recent (at that time) additions to their range, a blasting cabinet complete with gun and aluminium oxide medium. The all-in price of this outfit is around £600 and there is a cheaper bench—mounted version. This, like the parts washer, has become a permanent fixture at S.W. Classics.

I would suggest that any amateur who already possesses a suitable compressor (the cabinet requires 8cfm free air delivery at 100psi) and who anticipates carrying out restoration work for several years might well consider one of these cabinets. It should be even more affordable in a shared workshop.

Certainly it could save a great deal of ▶

● *The first part of the oil pump came away complete with the long bolts and here the rotors and housing are being lifted out as a separate assembly.*

● *Here the head is lying on its side on the bench. The right—hand valve is an exhaust valve complete with two—piece upper collar, the outer part of which is prone to cracking.*

● *Using a spring compressor to remove the valves. The ends of the valve stems may be slightly burred so that they will not pass easily through the valve guides. Don't force them but use a file to remove the burrs.*

● *There is a tendency for cracks to occur between the valve seats in the cylinder head where there is very little metal. This is most likely to happen in numbers one and two cylinders.*

● *Once washed, the components were laid out on clean paper to dry – very little cleaning fluid need be wasted.*

● *The blast cabinet: Compressed air is fed in through the hose near the bottom centre of the picture. A vacuum cleaner is connected to the cabinet (top right) to extract dust and thus remove the fog which would otherwise occur while work was in progress.*

● *The door of the cabinet hinges open to reveal the heavy-duty rubber gloves, the strong grille through which the blasting medium falls into the hopper beneath and, the gun with its two hoses (one for compressed air and the other rests in the hopper).*

● *The rocker cover demonstrates what can be achieved in a very few minutes in the blast cabinet. Appropriate components could be washed, blasted and painted in primer within an hour or so of dismantling.*

The principal clubs which specialise in the Triumph TR range are:
The TR Register, 271 High Street, Berkhamstead, Herts, HP4 1AA.
TR Drivers' Club, 39 Brook Street, Benson, Oxon, OX9 6LQ. Tel. 0491 35456.

● *The parts washer: If you cannot spare the floor space in your workshop you might consider the bench-mounted model. The flexible spout can be positioned exactly where it is needed. The supply of fluid to the pump can be obstructed by a heavy build—up of dirt in the bottom of the washer but the dirt can be wiped away almost without interrupting the cleaning operation.*

expense and time when compared with sending components away for blasting and paying for the service. However, the right accommodation is needed for both the blast cabinet and the parts washer. If an inflammable degreasing and cleaning agent is used in the parts washer, which is likely, then the washer should be housed well away from the area in which welding is carried out, that is, in a separate building. The blast cabinet should be kept well away from the areas in which mechanical assembly work and painting are carried out.

Odd pistons

It became obvious that our engine had been rebuilt previously but not very well. There were many odd bolts etc. We noted that the second piston ring should have been in the top slot and, as it is stepped to allow for the wear ridge in the bore, it should have been the other way up as well.

Three of the pistons appeared to be +0.020in and newer than the others which were the standard size. The big end bearings were 0.030in undersize. As Phil pointed out, there had been what you might call a "budget rebuild" at some time in the past. There was some wear on the gudgeon pins. We concluded that if the bores would hone satisfactorily the whole engine could be bored to +0.020in. The new parts which we planned to fit included valve guides, oil pump, camshaft and followers, rocker shaft and rockers. Existing valves would have to be re-faced because although they were high on their seatings their edges were hollow.

More about this next month when we will be rebuilding and timing the engine. ∎

TR6 RESTORATION

Part 8: Rebuilding and timing the engine. By John Williams.

● *The rear oil seal housing's mounting bolts were tightened in easy stages and while working diagonally — to minimise the risk of damage to the aluminium casting and to ensure that it did not move out of position while the bolts were being tightened.*

Our TR6 has been nearing completion at an increasing rate of knots lately. Recently S.W. Classics have been tackling engine, transmission and suspension work as well as painting and, probably because they needed a rest from me, I had a day out at Autotrim in Ivybridge where the TR6 seats were being rebuilt.

Our engine has been rebored and the head skimmed. The flywheel has been bead blasted and skimmed. A new crankshaft with matching big end bearings was obtained together with new pistons and small ends. Everything has been balanced including the clutch and flywheel. We have new valve guides and most of the valves are new too. The valve seats have been recut and those valves which were due to be re-used were resurfaced to eliminate some hollowness in their seating surfaces.

Hugh Roberts was given the task of rebuilding the engine and the following notes should be read in conjunction with the picture captions. As always you are recommended to refer to the workshop manual for torque and other settings.

Hugh's first job was to fit new core plugs, smearing each plug and its aperture in the block with a sealing compound such as Blue Hylomar or Hermetite.

The gudgeon pins and small end bushes were smeared with oil and the former proved to be "a sliding fit" in the pistons, so there was no need to heat the pistons when fitting them. One of the two gudgeon pin retaining circlips was fitted into its groove in each piston (before the gudgeon pin was inserted into the piston) to indicate how far to push the gudgeon pin into the piston. The gudgeon pin was then fitted through one side of the piston, through the small end bush of the connecting rod – with the connecting rod the correct way round – and on into the other side of the piston. When the gudgeon pin was in far enough the other retaining circlip was fitted.

TIMING

We fitted a Piper BP270 fast road camshaft to our TR6. Piper camshafts are supplied with fitting instructions and tables of timing figures and the latter informed us that the inlet valves should be on maximum lift at 112 degrees after TDC and that the valve clearances should be 0.012in inlet and 0.014in exhaust.

If, when the camshaft/crankshaft gear alignment is checked, the crankshaft gear needs to be moved away from the engine a little you can put shims behind it. If it is too far out then it is a matter of removing metal from the back of the gear by using the plate glass and grinding paste technique which is sometimes used to restore the flat surface to such items as small cylinder heads, oil pump covers etc.

Hugh adopted the same procedure for

timing the engine as he had used just over a year earlier on our Vitesse. Stage one was to position number one piston (the front one) at top dead centre and then turn the crankshaft until it was at 112 degrees after TDC. Stage two was to position the camshaft where number one inlet valve would be at its maximum lift. Finally, he had to keep both shafts in these positions while fitting the timing chain.

Top dead centre was found by using a

● Having started each core plug with very light hammer blows around its perimeter, a socket of suitable size was used as a drift. Each plug was tapped into its housing gently and very squarely until it was flush with the surface of the block.

● Each piston has to be fitted the right way round on the conrod and each piston's crown is marked "Front". With the conrod's bolts upwards, as shown here, the front of the piston is facing towards the bottom of the picture.

● Plenty of oil was used in the bores and the piston ring grooves, the ring gaps were spread around the perimeter of each piston and each conrod was aligned in the middle of its gudgeon pin before each piston/conrod assembly was lowered into its bore. Note the type of piston ring compressor recommended for this job

● Numbers are etched on the conrods and big end caps so that they should not be mixed and the main bearing caps are numbered too. Hugh put the big end shells into the conrods and the main bearing shells into their seatings in the block with generous doses of engine oil on both.

● Here the crankshaft is in position and oil is being applied to its bearing surfaces prior to fitting the bearing caps.

● One half-round thrust washer fits on each side of the block at the rear end of the crankshaft.

● With plenty of oil on the big end and main bearing caps, clean threads on the main bearing bolts and using new spring washers, the torque on the main bearing bolts should be 50-65lb/ft, on the big end shell bolts 38-46lb/ft, achieved in easy stages rather than all at once.

● Two very small gaskets were stuck in place with grease adjacent to the front main bearing cap before the sealing block was fitted followed by the wooden filling pieces. The latter should be driven into their apertures at each end of the sealing block and excess wood trimmed off flush with a sharp blade.

● Again, grease was used to stick the front engine plate gasket in place and on the front plate itself.

● *A straight-edge was used to check the alignment of the timing gears. Then the camshaft gear was removed while the engine was timed.*

● *This picture, from our earlier series on the Vitesse, shows the dial gauge and timing disc in position ready to find true top dead centre. Note the long bolt fitted adjacent to the timing disc – the head of the bolt has a line scribed across it to act as a pointer.*

● *Here the dial gauge is working on the cam follower extension as described in the text.*

● *Note that the concave side of the oil thrower faces away from the engine. Next, a spacer fits over the crankshaft and it is against this that the timing cover oil seal bears.*

● *The unusual variety of nuts, bolts and screws used when fitting the timing cover: It looks like an odd assortment but this is correct.*

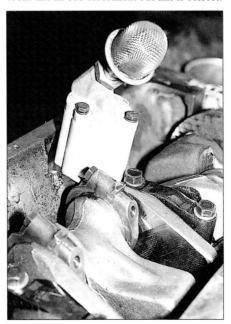

● *Plenty of oil should be applied to the internal components of the oil pump before fitting it – whether it is new or not.*

timing disc on the front of the crankshaft in conjunction with a mark on an adjacent bolt head as a pointer and a dial gauge which was set up to measure the movement of the piston crown. First, the crankshaft was turned until number one piston was (as near as could be judged by eye) at top dead centre. Then the timing disc reading was set to zero, as was the dial gauge. Then the crankshaft was rotated slightly until a reading of 10thou was indicated on the gauge and at this point a note was made of the timing disc reading. The exact dial gauge reading doesn't matter so long as the same figure is used throughout the procedure. Then the crankshaft was rotated the opposite way until the dial gauge reading was 10thou again and, once more, a note was made of the timing disc reading. Then the crankshaft was turned again until the timing disc gave a reading halfway between the previous two readings and number one piston was now at true top dead centre. Then, by reference to the timing disc, it was a simple matter to rotate the crankshaft until it was at the required 112 degrees after TDC.

CAMSHAFT LIFT

Next we carried out a similar exercise to find the position of the camshaft at which the number one inlet valve would be at maximum lift. Hugh used a home-made extension which fitted the cam follower and enabled the dial gauge (placed on top of the block) to measure the movement of the cam follower. We found the approximate maximum lift position by hand and then set the dial gauge at zero. Keeping a finger on the extension (to simulate the effect of a valve spring) we rotated the camshaft using, as handles, a couple of long bolts into the holes in its flange. When the dial gauge indicated 10thou we used paint to mark both the camshaft flange and the adjacent retaining plate. Then we rotated the camshaft the opposite way until a reading of 10thou was indicated again – and made another mark on the retaining plate opposite that on the camshaft flange. Now, by turning the camshaft so that the mark on its flange was halfway between the two marks on the retaining plate we found the true maximum lift position of number one inlet valve.

Next the timing chain was put around the camshaft sprocket (not yet attached to the camshaft) and fed over the crankshaft sprocket (which had been on the crankshaft throughout the timing procedure) and this was repeated a few times until two of the holes in the camshaft sprocket lined up precisely with two of the camshaft flange holes. This has to be done with care to avoid rotating either the camshaft or the crankshaft. Then the camshaft sprocket was bolted to the camshaft flange and the tabs on the locking washer were turned over.

REAR OIL SEAL

The rear oil seal was fitted into its housing by tapping it in gently on a flat bench with a soft mallet. Then oil was applied to the inner circumference of the oil seal and to the crankshaft so that it was not assembled dry. A paper gasket fits between the oil seal housing and the rear of the crankcase and this was held in place by a smear of

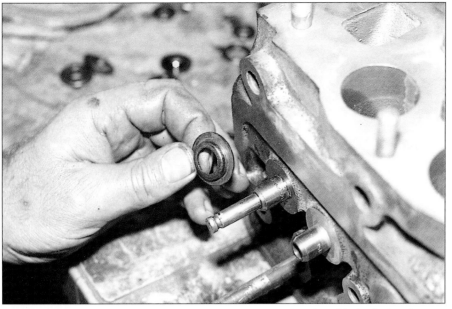

● *This was the type of lower spring collar which we used in conjunction with the single valve springs.*

● *Oil was applied to the valve stems before putting them in the guides and the valves were ground in.*

● *The corresponding wear inside the rocker from the damaged part of the shaft in the earlier picture. The rockers were renewed.*

● *Our old rocker shaft (bottom) displaying the classic wear pattern – compare it with the same section of the new shaft above.*

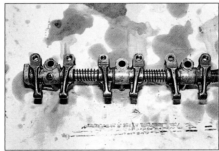

● *These two pictures show the order in which the parts fit on the rocker shaft and which way round the inlet and exhaust rockers fit. Note the extra thick spacer washers of which there are four (arrowed A) and there are two spring washers (arrowed B).*

grease. Another light smear was put on the housing itself.

Though we fitted a new oil pump we dismantled and reassembled it immediately prior to fitting and applied plenty of oil to its internal components.

CYLINDER HEAD

Double valve springs are the norm on the standard TR6 engine but our Piper fast road camshaft required single uprated springs. These in turn called for a different type of lower spring collar so that the single springs would seat correctly.

Theoretically it should have been possible to slide everything off the rocker shaft once the screw in the rearmost pedestal had been undone. Our pedestal had seized to the shaft, as had the next one along. So we removed the split-pin at the other end of the shaft and started there. The important thing is to keep all the components in the right order as they are removed from the shaft or, at least, to devise some means of ensuring that you put them back in the correct order.

We used a new rocker shaft and rockers. When using a new shaft it is well worth checking that the core plugs have been fitted at both ends – sometimes they are forgotten. A new split-pin was fitted to the new shaft and all the rockers, spacers, springs and pedestals were laid out in the correct order and fed on to the new shaft using plenty of oil. If, for any reason, you are required to part with the old rockers, remember to remove the adjusters from them as new rockers do not come with adjusters.

Next month we will have a look at the sort of repairs which our wheel arches required.

The companies who have been involved in this TR6 project so far are:

S.W. Classics, Brook House, Dartington, nr Totnes, Devon. Tel: (0803) 865842.
Machine Mart Limited, 211 Lower Parliament Street, Nottingham, NG1 1GN. Tel: (0602) 587666.
Abbot Blasting of Newton Abbot, Bradley Lane, Newton Abbot. Tel: 68684.
GEM Developments, Beacon Park, Plymouth. Tel. 0752 705989.
Clive Manvers, Unit 1, Buttons Green Farm, Cockfield, Bury St Edmunds, Suffolk, IP30 0JF. Tel. 0284 828674. Fax: 0284 827063.
Rimmer Bros Ltd, Triumph House, Sleaford Road, Bracebridge Heath, Lincoln, LN4 2NA. Tel. 0522 568000, fax. 0522 567600.
TR Bitz, Lyncastle Way, Barley Castle Trading Estate, Appleton, Warrington, Cheshire, WA4 4ST. Tel. 0925 861861, fax. 0925 860816.

The principal clubs which specialise in the Triumph TR range are:

The TR Register, 271 High Street, Berkhamstead, Herts, HP4 1AA.
TR Drivers' Club, 39 Brook Street, Benson, Oxon, OX9 6LQ. Tel. 0491 35456.

TR6 RESTORATION

Part 10: The gearbox overhaul by John Williams

Our TR6 is being painted as I write this month's episode and when these words are published the car will have been finished for some time. However, there is plenty of ground which has yet to be covered in these articles and this month I am continuing the mechanical theme by showing some of the work which was done by S. W. Classics (telephone 0803 8G5842) on the transmission.

Chris Bass was given the task of sorting the gearbox and overdrive and his first job was to remove the top cover. Having noted that a new switch would be need to replace one which had snapped off in the cover, the first thing we looked for was wear in the selector arms. All the components in the cover were dismantled for cleaning and inspection. This, and reassembly, is straightforward but there are a couple of points worth mentioning here. First, there is a row of threaded caps along the front flange of the cover. These caps are slotted so that they can be unscrewed by a

screwdriver. Under each cap is a spring, a ball and a plunger. The caps need removing with care so as not to lose any of these small items and note the order which they come out so that you will put them back in the right order.

Secondly, there is a hole in the bottom of the gearlever which accommodates a spring and a plunger. These were designed to eliminate gearlever vibration in conjunction with adjusting screws on either side of the gearlever housing. To arrive at the correct adjustment put the spring and plunger into the gearlever and the gearlever into its housing. Move the gearlever into the lst/2nd gear plane, turn the screw on that side until it just touches the bottom of the gearlever, back it off half a turn then tighten the locknut. Then, engage reverse gear and do the same on that side.

The clutch operating shaft assembly was removed from the bell housing next. A square-headed screw locks the clutch operating fork on to the shaft and the shaft itself was retained by a screw through the offside rear of the bell housing.

The overdrive is attached to the gearbox by studs and nuts around the perimeter of the casing including an extra long stud on each side. The latter enable the tension of the springs within the overdrive to be released gradually as the overdrive and gearbox are separated.

It was very cold on the days on which this work was being done and, by mid-afternoon, after a long spell with the workshop doors open, we decided to try out a couple of workshop heaters from Machine Mart. In fact we tried them on separate days and the first of them was the Easi-Heat 145 propane fired space heater. The output of this machine is variable within the range 25,000 to 140,000 Btu/hour and the manufacturers suggest that the cubic capacity (in cubic feet) of a reasonably well insulated building multiplied by five, will give the B.T.U. requirement to raise the temperature by 20 degrees F.

We were very impressed by this heater and turned it off after 20 minutes or 80 because the workshop (which I estimated to be around 6,000-7,000 cubic feet though certainly not well insulated) was quite warm enough. This was a most effective heater which was quite obviously able to heat much larger workshops. At £289 + VAT it 18 not one of the cheaper pieces of workshop equipment.

What we needed to try out was a heater suitable for the DiY restorer whose workshop might be about the size of a decent double garage or perhaps a little larger, say 3,000-6,000 cubic feet. Machine Mart supplied a Clarke "Little Devil" heater. Its maximum output was quoted as 10Kw, ie 33,000Btu per hour "for areas of up to 5,000 cubic feet."

❶ *As with any other mechanical work the secret of success with a gearbox/ overdrive assembly is to work in an orderly way, separating major assemblies first, then sub-assemblies, and keeping components in order within their groups.*

TR6 RESTORATION

Again this was a very effective heater, unbelievably so, in view of its small size. Its price was £129.95 + VAT. If you have spent a small fortune equipping a decent workshop yet feel disinclined to use it in the winter months because it is too cold this could solve your problem.

The next job on the gearbox was to remove the front cover inside the bellhousing (four screws), including the oil seal which was renewed later.

Then the overdrive adapter plate was removed from the rear of the gearbox as was the locking plate for the countershaft and reverse gear shaft. Someone had used a chisel at some time previously on the Posidrive screw securing the locking plate.

In the bellhousing the small cover (2 screws) was removed and the layshaft was pushed out allowing its gears to drop into the bottom of the box.

A circlip and washer were removed from the rear end of the mainshaft then the input (constant pinion) shaft was drifted out in a forward direction by applying the drift to the front bearing from within the box - making sure to recover the spigot bearing from its housing inside the rear end of the input shaft assembly.

To remove the rear bearings from the mainshaft the first step was to drive the shaft forward slightly into the box. Then the bearing was drifted backwards out of the casing until it could slip off the shaft. Then the shaft itself (complete with all its gears etc.) could be tilted upwards, if the various components on it were held together in a tight group, and lifted out of the top of the box.

Next the reverse gear shaft was pushed out of the back of the casing and the gear removed from the box. Then the thrust washer was extracted from behind the laygear cluster in the bottom of the box and the cluster itself was lifted out.

It may seem obvious but if you want your gearbox to be as new then you must replace any component that is even slightly worn, even if it is judged to be re-usable. If you obtain reconditioned box you cannot necessarily assume that all wearing parts will have been renewed. A reconditioned box could contain various components which are not strictly TR6 parts (some may come from the 2000/2500/2.5 range of saloons) and our box, whose history is unknown, showed a few variations of this sort - which are by no means unusual.

Cleanliness is important when working on gearboxes and overdrive units and, once again, the Machine Mart parts washer made an otherwise tedious job relatively pleasant and easy. After cleaning, the parts were laid out in an orderly fashion on clean paper on the bench ready for reassembly.

All components were examined closely. Our plan was to replace all bearings together with any other parts which appeared worn or damaged. The latter included the input shaft synchro, the large gear on the front of the laygear cluster from which one tooth had broken off (and was found in the bottom of the box) and, the circlip which retains third gear on the mainshaft. It was necessary to remove this circlip when dismantling the components of the mainshaft and, once removed; it should not be reused.

Our layshaft assembly required new needle

2 *The selector forks were examined for wear end here one of the caps is being threaded back into front flange - far enough to take on some spring loading and to be at least flush with the flange.*

3 *The adjusting screws and locknuts which are used to take up excess movement in the gearlever can be seen on each side of the gearlever housing.*

4 *Note the extra long stud at the overdrive/gearbox flanges (there is one on the other side too) to allow the internal spring pressure to be released gradually.*

5 *Having loosened all the nuts Chris tapped the casing with a mallet to break the seal..Overdrive is the 'A' type.*

6 *With the four bolts removed the front cover (nosepiece) was free to slide off the input shaft complete with the oil seal which it contains. The lower cover came off later to release the layshaft.*

rollers at both ends and a replacement for a badly shipped constant gear. Within each end of the layshaft assembly circlips were removed 80 that the needle roller bearings behind them could be replaced by new ones. Behind each bearing was a tapered ring which stayed in place.

When refitting the layshaft assembly to the box we put the forward thrust washer in first, holding it in place with grease, then the layshaft assembly followed by the rear thrust washer. All of this rested in the bottom of the box until the reverse gear shaft and mainshaft were in place. Later the box was turned upside down so that the layshaft assembly would fall into position for its shaft to be inserted.

To fit a new bearing to the input shaft Chris removed a circlip from the shaft then supported the old bearing on a vice while he drove the shaft through the bearing using a mallet and a piece of hardwood. An oil thrower fits on the input shaft between the gear and the bearing and the shaft had to be driven through the new bearing far enough to allow a washer and a circlip to be fitted. The bearing itself must

7 *The cam which drives the overdrive pump simply slides off the mainshaft and, when refitted, the thinnest part of the cam should be towards the bottom of the box.*

The companies who have been involved in this TR6 project so far are:
S. W. Classics, Brook House, Dartington, Nr Totnes, Devon. Tel: (0803) 865842.
Machine Mart Limited, 211 Lower Parliament Street, Nottingham NGI 1GN. Tel: (0602) 587666.
Abbot Blasting of Newton Abbot, Bradley Lane, Newton Abbot. Tel: 68684.
GEM Developments, Beacon Park, Plymouth. Tel. 0752 705989.
J and B. T. Engineering, Unit 3 Brook House, Dartington, Totnes, Devon TQ9 6DJ.
Clive Manvers, Unit 1 Buttons Green Farm, Cockfield, Bury St Edmunds, Suffolk, IP30 OJf. Tel. 0284 828674. Fax: 0284 827063.
Rimmer Bros Ltd, Triumph House, Sleaford Road, Bracebridge Heath, Lincoln, LN4 2NA. Tel. 0522 568000, Fax. 0522 567600.
TR Bitz, Lyncastle Way, Barley Castle Trading Estate, Appleton, Warrington, Cheshire, WA4 45T. Tel. 0925 861861, Fax. 0925 860816.

8 *Why it is important to examine components carefully - it is easy to miss a chipped gear, even one as bad as this.*

9 *A little oil was applied to the shaft before the new gear was fitted.*

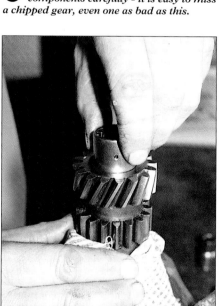

10 *A new needle roller assembly was needed for each end of the layshaft and (if you have had your three Weetabix) these can be pressed in by hand.*

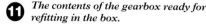

11 *The contents of the gearbox ready for refitting in the box.*

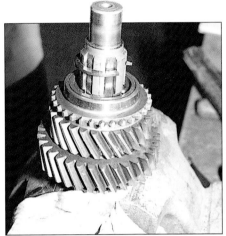

12 *Using a feeler gauge to check the layshaft assembly end float. 8-12 thou between the thrust washer and the laygear.*

13 *The reverse gear and shaft in position and located on the change lever.*

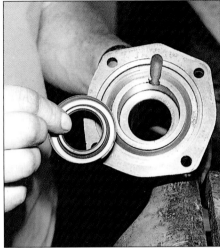

19 *A new oil seal for the nosepiece. Note the oilway in the nosepiece casting*

14 *Note the oil thrower washer between the gear and the bearing on the input shaft.*

15 *The new circlip being placed on the mainshaft assembly between second and third gear.*

16 *The mainshaft and input shaft assemblies: The latter with its bearing is on the right and the bearing for the rear end of the mainshaft was fitted after the shaft was placed back in the box.*

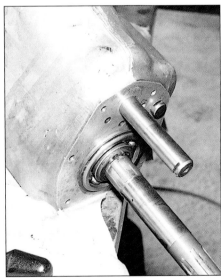

17 *With the gearbox upside down and the mainshaft and input shaft assemblies already in position, the layshaft cluster should drop into the correct position for its shaft to be inserted.*

18 *The bearing on the rear end of the mainshaft has a circlip around its perimeter outside the gearbox casing and there is a washer and a circlip on the shaft itself. The small plate, secured by a Posidrive screw, locks the layshaft and reverse gear shaft in their respective positions.*

TR6 RESTORATION

be fitted the right way around as a groove around its perimeter accommodates another circlip which in turn rests against the outside of the gearbox casing

The various parts on the mainshaft proved to be in good condition and we replaced the circlip (mentioned earlier) and the bearing. If you are unfamiliar with the internals of the gearbox you will find it vital to keep parts in the correct order throughout and particularly when dealing with the seemingly intimidating array of parts which fit on the mainshaft. In fact there are no real difficulties here. It is just a matter of noting which way round and in what order various items come off the shaft so that you will know how to put them back.

After reassembly, the mainshaft was returned to the gearbox and the new bearing fitted to its rear end complete with a retaining circlip around its perimeter, followed by a washer around the shaft and a circlip which located in a slot around the shaft. The input shaft had been fitted to the box by this stage and the box was turned up on to its front end so that the front end of the input shaft was on a block of wood on the floor. Then a metal tube was placed over the rear end of the mainshaft and this was used to drift the bearing into its housing in the casing.

One final point: When refitting the nosepiece inside the bell housing, it is vital that it (and its gasket) are the right way round so that the oilway aligns with the hole adjacent to the bearing in the bell housing casting which is actually on the~ offside of the input shaft. Also, the splines on the input shaft should be greased before fitting the nosepiece to help prevent damage to the oil seal which it contains.

NEXT MONTH: Overdrive and diff. ■

The principal clubs which specialise in the Triumph TR range are:
The TR Register, 271 High Street, Berkhamstead, Herts, HP4 1AA.
TR Drivers' Club, 39 Brook Street, Benson, Oxon, OX9 6LQ. Tel. 0491 35458.

1 *Blue Hylomar was used very sparingly to hold the gasket in place before the overdrive was refitted to the gearbox - avoiding at all costs any risk of excess sealant getting into the overdrive.*

2 *We removed the cover plate then slackened the pinch bolt and removed the solenoid lever, followed by the housing, which was spring loaded by the accumulator spring...*

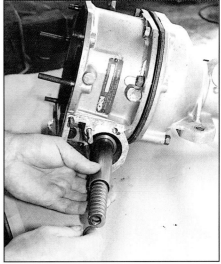

3 *...this was followed by the spring and spacer tube.*

TR6 RESTORATION

Part 11: Rebuilding the overdrive and differential by John Williams

There was no particular reason to anticipate problems in our overdrive or differential, but both were dismantled sufficiently to allow inspection and the replacement of worn parts.

If there has been a gearbox problem which has resulted in particles of metal getting into the oil (which is shared with the overdrive) it is worth cleaning out the overdrive, even though it may not need an overhaul. The notes which follow should be read in conjunction with a workshop manual and I leave it to individual readers to decide for themselves whether they have the necessary equipment and expertise to tackle complete overhauls of overdrives and rear axles.

The solenoid was missing from our 'A' type overdrive at the outset and its mounting arrangement was of the Triumph 2000 type which has a housing enclosing the solenoid lever. As I pointed out last month, it is not unusual to find variations of this sort now that there has been ample time for reconditioned units to have been fitted to these cars.

In the interests of safety it is worth mentioning again that when separating the overdrive from the gearbox, the long bolts should not be removed until the joint at the gasket has been broken and the tension of the overdrive springs has been released gradually - even if the overdrive appears to stick to the gearbox after all bolts have been slackened. ▶

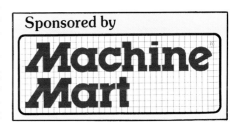

4 *Chris used this special tool to extract the accumulator housing and piston assembly. When the rubber washer built into the tool is inserted into the piston, then compressed by turning the threaded rod within the centre of the tool, the diameter of the washer increases and grips the piston.*

6 *The overdrive's circular bottom cover was removed together with its magnetic washers (which are there to pick up swarf) and filter.*

7 *The bottom of the pump operating mechanism which can be seen when the circular cover is removed. There should be no need to disturb this mechanism.*

5 *The nuts and washers were removed to release the bridge pieces at the open end of the overdrive.*

8 *The forward section of the overdrive casing and assembly was removed next then . . .*

9 *. . . the brake ring was lifted off - having been eased with a soft mallet.*

TR6 RESTORATION

We started by taking off the solenoid lever cover plate and then continued as shown in the pictures looking for wear or damage. For example, it was important to examine the accumulator housing and piston assembly, which might have become scored, or the 'O' ring may have deteriorated. The nuts around the perimeter of the casing were undone evenly to split the casing. With the casing secured tail downwards in a vice (and protected from the vice by a pad of soft material) the brake ring, thrust ring and clutch assemblies were lifted off.

By this stage the planet wheel assembly was exposed and though this can be lifted out, it is vital to note before doing so that there are punch marks on the planet wheels which show exactly where they should mesh with the sun wheel and they must be reassembled in the same position.

The annulus assembly includes the shaft which passes through the rear of the overdrive casing to the flange and castellated nut on the outside. In the centre of the annulus is the sun wheel and behind this is the unidirectional clutch. Both of these can be lifted out together with various adjusting washers and thrust washers.

The unidirectional clutch is likely to fall apart as it is taken out and, in the absence of the special tool for reinstating it, you will have to do the best you can with strong rubber bands to hold it all together during reassembly. A screw on the side of the casing secures the speedometer drive, which has to be taken out before the annulus assembly.

The latter can be driven forward out of the casing (using a soft mallet) after the castellated nut, washer and flange have been removed from the rear end. This leaves an oil seal and a bearing within the casing and these have to be pushed out towards the rear.

I would suggest that unless the overdrive is unusually badly worn and needs new bearings, thrust washers and readjustment of the annulus end-float, it would be worth avoiding dismantling beyond the planet gears any more than is necessary to wash out the rear of the unit.

Our overdrive was reassembled with gearbox oil to make everything slide easily and to keep it free of rust until it was in use again. New spring washers were used all

10 *The clutch assembly coming out. The lining material was in good condition.*

The companies who have been involved in this TR6 project so far are:
S. W. Classics, Brook House, Dartington, Totnes, Devon. Tel: (0803) 865842.
Machine Mart Limited, 211 Lower Parliament Street, Nottingham NGl 1GN. Tel: (0602) 587666.
Abbot Blasting , Bradley Lane, Newton Abbot. Tel: 0626 68684.
GEM Developments, Beacon Park, Plymouth. Tel. 0752 705989.
J and B. T. Engineering, Unit 3, Brook House, Dartington, Totnes, Devon TQ9 6DJ.
Clive Manvers, Unit 1 Buttons Green Farm, Cockfield, Bury St Edmunds, Suffolk, IP30 OJF. Tel: 0284 828674. Fax: 0284 827063.
Revington TR Spares, Home Farm, Middlezoy, Bridgwater, Somerset. Tel: 0283 69437. Fax: 0823 698109.
Rimmer Bros Ltd, Triumph House, Sleaford Road, Bracebridge Heath, Lincoln, LN4 2NA. Tel. 0522 568000, Fax. 0522 567600.
TR Bitz, Lyncastle Way, Barley Castle Trading Estate, Appleton, Warrington, Cheshire, WA4 45T. Tel. 0925 861861, Fax. 0925 860816.
TR GB, 3 Warner's Drove, Somersham, Huntingdon, Cambridgeshire, PE17 3HW. Tel: 0487 842168. Fax: 0487 740274.

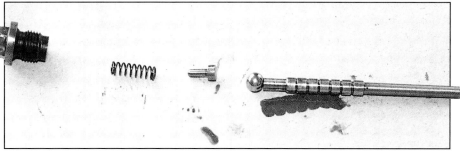

12 *The operating valve's components in (left to right) the order in which they came out of the housing...*

11 *The oil pump valve consists of a hexagonal plug with sealing washer, a small spring and piston and a ball bearing. The valve's housing is alongside the accumulator assembly.*

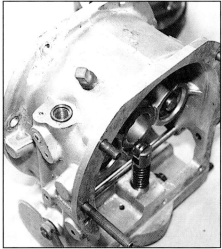

13 *...which is located on the upper offside of the overdrive casing.*

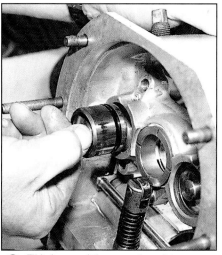

14 *This is one of the operating pistons, complete with 'O' ring, which we removed for inspection.*

round. The gearbox was supported on its front end on thick wooden blocks on the floor and the cam, which drives the overdrive pump, was placed on the output shaft with its thinnest part facing towards the bottom of the box.

A loop of wire was fitted around the overdrive's pump plunger so that the plunger could be lifted on to the cam and the wire retrieved afterwards. The overdrive was lowered on to the gearbox and the overdrive springs were fed into position, the four shorter ones towards the centre of the overdrive and all eight located correctly on the adaptor plate. In theory, having lifted the pump plunger on to the cam, the overdrive can be pulled into position against the gearbox by using the long screw on each side of the housing until it is possible to insert the short screws.

Our differential was overhauled by Bill Tolley, of J and B.T. Engineering, whose workshop is next door to S.W. Classics at Brook House, Dartington. Our brief was to examine the diff. and replace any worn parts.

Having removed the cover on the rear of the casing, followed by the inner axle shaft bearing retainers on both sides of the casing, the inner axle shafts were withdrawn from the casing and Bill turned his attention to the differential unit itself.

The differential bearing caps were removed but Bill marked one of them so that it would go back later on the same side. A special spreading tool was needed to, in effect, distort the casing so that the differential could be extracted. This tight fit, possibly supplemented by shims (though not on our particular unit), was designed to apply the correct preload to the bearings. It is possible to extract the diff. assembly by using a couple of pairs of long, stout levers but great care must be taken to keep the assembly very "square" in relation to the casing otherwise it will jam.

The bearings on the differential assembly proved to be in good order as did the other components of this assembly. To change these bearings requires a two-legged puller with fairly narrow legs to fit the recesses behind the bearings - and a press with which to fit the new bearings.

If you dismount the crownwheel from the differential case flange, both crownwheel and flange should be marked first so that they can be reassembled in exactly the same position.

A dial gauge can be used to check "run-out" at the crownwheel mounting flange (minus crownwheel) and, later, at the teeth of the crownwheel. Run-out should not exceed 0.003in. If the mounting flange is within limits but the crownwheel is not, the cause could be dirt trapped behind the crownwheel or, burrs around the edges of bolt holes. ▶

15 *The eight springs - the four shorter ones to the centre of the unit - were refitted as the overdrive was lowered on to the gearbox.*

16 *If the overdrive and gearbox do not pull together smoothly, undue force should not be used. The cause may be simply a matter of misaligned splines.*

The principal clubs which specialise in the Triumph TR range are:
The TR Register, 271 High Street, Berkhamstead, Herts, HP4 1AA.
TR Drivers' Club, 39 Brook Street, Benson, Oxon, OX9 6LQ. Tel. 0491 35458.

bearings on either side of the crownwheel assembly. There weren't any shims in our assembly and, as nothing had been changed, there was no reason why we should have needed them during reassembly.

We removed the pinion assembly from the casing to examine the bearings for, among other things, pitting and other marks on the rollers and the races. Had the bearings needed to be renewed, specialist equipment would have been required to achieve the correct settings during reassembly. Fortunately they didn't need to be changed, so all we had to do was to install a new oil seal and rebuild the assembly as we found it complete with the same shims.

Prior to removing the assembly, Bill had measured the distance from the flat face on the end of the pinion to the cover flange on the rear of the casing by using a dial gauge in conjunction with a distance piece - a rectangular block of steel with regular faces. The specific measurement was not important. What mattered was that, with the same distance piece, the same measurement was obtained again later after reassembly.

Setting up the pinion

During reassembly Bill set up the pinion complete with its flange but minus the oil seal (the latter was fitted later after the correct settings had been made). A pinion which has been set up properly should need a torque of 15lb/ft to turn it after a torque of 120lb/ft has been applied to the pinion nut. The variable factor is the number of shims used: If there are too many, the pinion will be too loose, and if there are too few it will be too tight.

17 *Here one of the differential bearing caps is being removed, having been marked first. The inner axle shaft oil seal housing bolts to the square face on the casing facing the camera.*

18 *The pinion assembly with one of the bearings, the bearing spacer, and shims on both sides of the bearing spacer. The shims nearest to the threaded end of the pinion set the pre-load on the bearing.*

One of the inner axle shaft bearings was in a very poor condition so both of these were replaced. First, the shaft was driven out of its flange using a mallet in conjunction with a block of wood or aluminium with the flange supported on the vice. Then the press was used to drive the shaft out of the old bearing and into the new one, using aluminium packing between the press and the shaft and keeping everything square under the press to avoid damaging the shaft. The bearing fits against a slight step on the shaft and the dial on the press showed a sudden pressure increase as this point was reached.

When refitting the axle shaft assemblies to the main casing, there were no gaskets but Hylomar was used sparingly. New spring washers were used on the four bolts through each axle shaft oil seal housing and, though the manual indicates that these bolts should have a torque of 20lb/ft, there is insufficient space to use a torque wrench. The important thing is to avoid overtightening these bolts.

NEXT MONTH: WHEEL ARCHES AND BODY BUILDING.

19 *By this stage the oil seal together with the pinion splines had been smeared with oil to prevent damage and the seal fitted (open end leading). Here the mounting bracket was being bolted on, tightening the bolts to 38lb/ft; the pinion flange would be refitted afterwards.*

Provided that everything is kept square, and undue force is avoided, the differential assembly can be tapped gently into the casing with the aid of a copper mallet, "expanding" the casing to the very slight extent required as it goes in. When the differential assembly is far enough into the casing it is possible to fit the bearing caps, tightening the cap bolts evenly in the manner of a cylinder head a little at a time to a torque of 38lb/ft.

While this is happening, the crownwheel should be checked frequently to ensure that it will turn still and is not locking up. The crownwheel can be moved to one side or the other if necessary to adjust the backlash (the degree of movement of the crownwheel within the pinion) by means of shims which go between the outer casing and the main

TR6 RESTORATION

Part 12: Wheel arch repairs and start of the body rebuild. Report by John Williams.

This month's story starts with some lightweight repairs to the wheelarches and ends with the massive task of rebuilding the body, which will be concluded next month.

The rear wheelarches were among the very few panels to be salvaged from the original bodywork of our TR6 and they had suffered typical rust damage at their front and rear lower edges. Replacement wheelarches were believed to be unobtainable when we reached this stage in the restoration early in 1991, but even if they had been available we may well have chosen to repair the originals.

The edges of the nearside wheelarch had rusted away. To obtain an approximate guide to the size and shape of the repair sections needed, John Holmes (at S.W. Classics) aligned the wheelarch with a new rear quarter panel then made the repair sections an inch or so oversize. The surplus metal would be trimmed off later at the bodywork building stage. The pictures show how the repairs were carried out, starting at the front of the panel.

Rebuilding the body

Watching good professional restorers at work, as I do for days at a time, tends to create the overwhelming impression that their work is easy. In fact it is highly skilled work and it is also mentally and physically tiring. It looks easy because the professionals are welding, panelbeating, fabricating etc. daily.

Just as sheer practice has made them the masters of their workshop equipment and techniques, it has also enabled them to anticipate and solve problems seemingly effortlessly. Amateur restorers have proved time and again that they too can achieve a

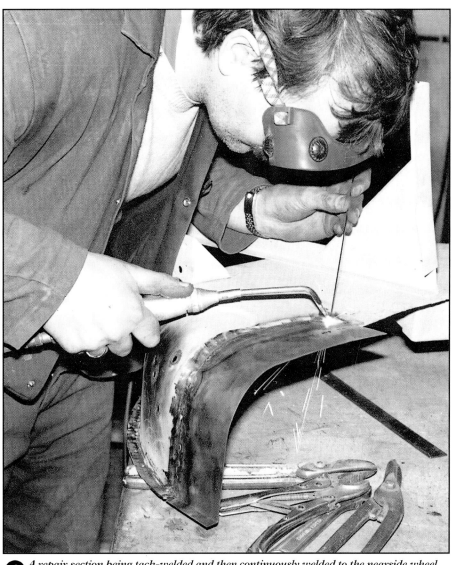

1 *A repair section being tack-welded and then continuously welded to the nearside wheel arch. Gloves should always be worn when welding - but many professionals don't.*

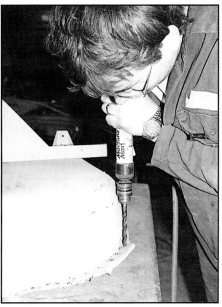

2 *Remnants of the adjacent panels were attached to the wheelarches still and these had to be removed by identifying, drilling and breaking the spot welds, peeling the remnants away using a combination of hammer and chisel and pliers as necessary . .*

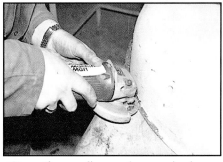

3 *. . . then sanding . . . (once again gloves should really be worn)*

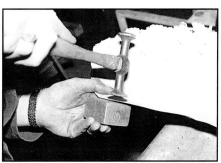

4 *. . . and planishing to make good the flanges.*

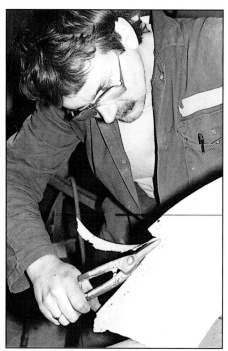

6 *The nearside wheelarch, showing the rusted rear end (right), some remnants of the original quarter panel attached to the flange and the front end (left) where rusted metal has been cut out.*

7 *An oblong piece of steel was cut and its edge was folded to make a flange. Then a straight edge was used to align the repair section as shown here...*

5 *Snips were used to cut out the rusted area at the front of the wheelarch.*

TR6 RESTORATION

8 *... before it was clamped into place and then scribed - using the edge of the previously cut wheelarch to guide the scriber. Surplus metal was cut off the repair section, then it was sanded and planished on the anvil and minor adjustments were made until it fitted perfectly.*

9 *Then the repair section was clamped in place again and several small tack welds were made, with frequent planishing in between, before it was continuously welded to the wheelarch. Take care when doing this - it's easy to cause distortion.*

very high degree of proficiency in various restoration skills now that good equipment is so readily available through firms such as Machine Mart.

The wheelarch repairs described this month, for example, should pose no problems for such amateurs but building a complete car body, and perhaps especially one which contains such a high proportion of reproduction panels as our TR6, is another matter altogether and certainly not a job for the fainthearted.

It is arguable that rebuilding a complete car body from end to end is the most difficult restoration task. Unlike a mechanical overhaul, for example, the work cannot be broken down into a series of precisely defined procedures. Panels, whether original, repaired or reproduction, will not necessarily fit satisfactorily without a fair amount of adjustment of one sort or another and neither is it reasonable to expect a motley selection of all three types of panels to fall together easily into the three-dimensional jigsaw of a car's body. I do not deny the existence of poor reproduction panels but it is a fact that many amateur restorers expect too much of the replacements on which they have spent their hard-earned cash, underestimating the importance of the essential ability to work metal, including "new" panels, to achieve the desired result.

Then there is the matter of trial-fitting. A great deal of time and trouble may be taken in clamping everything together so that it fits well and looks right and, though this is essential too, it does not guarantee the end result. After dismantling as necessary to create access for the final welding, the difficulties

10 *Finally, the repaired area was sanded clean to produce the now-familiar invisible repair.*

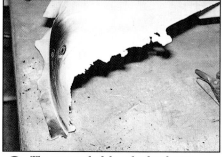

11 *The rear end of the wheelarch was repaired in a similar way. The rusted area was cut out but not scrapped.*

The companies who have been involved in this TR6 project so far are:
S. W. Classics, Brook House, Dartington, Nr Totnes, Devon. Tel: (0803) 865842.
Machine Mart Limited, 211 Lower Parliament Street, Nottingham NGl 1GN. Tel: (0602) 587666.
Autotrim, Filham Moor Industrial Estate, Ivybridge, Devon. Tel: 0752 893368.
Abbot Blasting of Newton Abbot, Bradley Lane, Newton Abbot. Tel: 68684.
GEM Developments, Beacon Park, Plymouth. Tel. 0752 705989.
J and B. T. Engineering, Unit 3 Brook House, Dartington, Totnes, Devon TQ9 6DJ.
Clive Manvers, Unit 1 Buttons Green Farm, Cockfield, Bury St Edmunds, Suffolk, IP30 OJf. Tel. 0284 828674. Fax: 0284 827063.
Revington TR Spares, Home Farm, Middlezoy, Bridgwater, Somerset, TA7 0PD. Tel: 0823 69437. Fax: 698109.
Rimmer Bros Ltd, Triumph House, Sleaford Road, Bracebridge Heath, Lincoln, LN4 2NA. Tel. 0522 568000, Fax. 0522 567600.
TR Bitz, Lyncastle Way, Barley Castle Trading Estate, Appleton, Warrington, Cheshire, WA4 45T. Tel. 0925 861861, Fax. 0925 860816.
TR GB, 3 Warners Drove, Somersham, Huntingdon, Cambridgeshire PE17 3HW. Tel: 0487 842168. Fax: 740274.

12 *An oversize repair section was made, complete with a short flange, curved to match the wheelarch and fitted carefully as shown here.*

15 *Nic Keeley (left) of Machine Mart is using a 5/16in UNF tap to clean the threads in the body mountings , while Stan Walters locates body mounting rubbers on the outriggers beneath the new floor panel to bring the level of the mounting brackets up to that of the chassis rails. Mounting brackets had been welded to the undersides of the floor panels earlier.*

13 *Then the old rusted metal was flattened and used as the pattern to guide the scriber when marking the curved edge shown here.*

14 *Finally the curved edge was cut with snips, leaving some excess metal to be trimmed off at the body building stage, and the welded area was sanded to complete the repair.*

experienced when trying to realign those panels which fitted so well previously can be immense.

This can be due to such invisible influences as the stresses which were in the panels prior to welding and the new ones created by the welding or, to the cumulative effect of stresses with one or more minor alterations in the realignment of the panels.

Reference points

The preparation for rebuilding the body should start before it is dismantled. Measurements should be taken and noted, as many as possible in fact. Sort out the fixed parts of the car from the movable panels. Usually the former will include suspension mounting points on the chassis and one or both of the bulkheads, while the wings, for example, are movable.

When taking measurements, use the fixed parts as reference points as far as possible. Measure the apertures for the doors, bonnet and bootlid if the panels are sound enough and the gaps satisfactory but, when rebuilding, bear in mind that you should adjust the apertures to suit the panels which occupy them, not the other way round - unless of course you have made an awful mess of reskinning a door or have bought a really disastrous reproduction bootlid, which has been known to happen. As the bodywork comes together, take measurements along both sides of the car at frequent intervals to ensure that the dimensions remain the same.

The account which follows gives a broad outline of the order in which our TR6 body ▶

16 *The front bulkhead was clamped into place next so that it aligned at its front edge with the front edge of the floor panels. It was also clamped to the chassis front side bracing members complete with the required mounting pads.*

TR6 RESTORATION

was reassembled together with a fair amount of detail. It does not and cannot provide a definitive set of instructions which guarantee a perfect completed body. This part in a restoration cannot be described in that way because it entails an enormous amount of trial and error and countless almost subconscious decisions, minor adjustments and alterations at every stage in the assembly work - and no two cars will produce quite the same assortment of problems.

On the TR6 only a limited amount of welding can be done until the car is virtually complete with all door and bonnet gaps etc. correct. Until then many panels have to be clamped into place at least initially. The inner sills can be welded into position but the outer sills are the last panels to be fitted, their precise location being arranged to suit the doors when everything else is in place.

The bodywork must be rebuilt on the chassis, working from front to rear after the bulkheads and floors are in place with the inner sills. So we started with the floor panels, which were reproductions, and the bulkheads, the rear one of which had been virtually made from scratch at S.W. Classics.

Next we turned our attention to the front wheelarches and closing panels, as shown in the pictures. More about this next month.

NEXT MONTH: FINISHING THE BODY REBUILD.

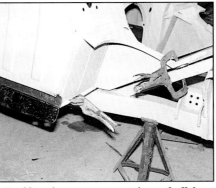

17 *Next the corners were trimmed off the lower front panels of the bulkhead so that the inner sills could protrude through them and the inner sills were fitted and tack-welded along their inner edges to the floor panels, ensuring that they remained flush with the floor panels on the outside.*

19 *The closing panels were removed and the wheelarches were clamped into place and tack-welded.*

18 *The front wheelarch closing panels (reproductions) were trial-fitted and needed some adjustment to make them fit right back against the bulkhead.*

One jump ahead

Readers who have been following the TR rebuild series may have noticed that we jumped from Part 8 to 10 - there is no Part 9. We apologise for any confusion.

TR6 RESTORATION

Part 13: Finishing the bodywork rebuild. John Williams reports.

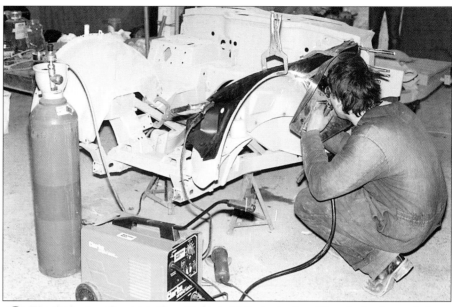

1 *The closing panels were tack-welded around the perimeter of the wheelarches and also on the bulkhead flanges. Note the Argoshield bottle connected to the Clarke 120E MIG welder supplied by the project's sponsors, Machine Mart - a vast improvement on those small bottles which come as standard accessories.*

Last month's story ended when we began to fit the front wheel arches and closing panels. These were followed by the outer wings and the bonnet. When these were in place and the gaps at the sides and rear of the bonnet were satisfactory, the trial fitting was extended to include the doors so that the gaps at their leading edges could be sorted out. With this done, the bonnet was checked again to ensure that its gaps and its position in relation to the front of the wings was satisfactory still.

When the seat pan assembly was installed on the chassis its rear part should have been vertical, forming, in effect, the front of the spare wheel well. We found that the reinforcing brackets on the rear face of the bridge (which incorporates the rearmost diff. mountings) prevented this because they protruded too far to the rear.

This whole bridge assembly was bought in as a reproduction part - the original having been missing from our chassis. To solve the problem we cut the lower part of each of these reinforcing brackets and flattened the brackets against the bridge to which they were then welded. The seat pan then fitted properly, matching up with the boot floor. The hole in the centre of the boot floor has to align with the spare wheel mounting on the chassis cross tube. Incidentally, TR6 boot floor panels were unobtainable so we modified a TR4 panel.

We put the boot floor in place at an early stage and the next step was to install the rear wheel arches, quarter panels, the rear deck, the outer wings and the rear valance assembly. The rear lower panel was installed earlier with our boot floor and the upper reinforcement panel would be installed later. ▶

Sponsored by

2 *This "big bottle adaptor" (from Machine Mart) has a pressure gauge but not a flow gauge. A similar adaptor, but without a pressure gauge, is available for use on standard Co2 bottles..*

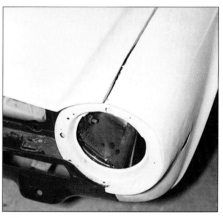

3 *The front panel was tack-welded on (there was no room for clamps), the wings bolted on, the bonnet fitted and the alignment of the wings and bonnet was adjusted so that the gaps were right and they matched above the headlamp apertures.*

4 *Now the doors were added and their front gaps adjusted. Note that the bottoms of the 'A' posts are split to pass on both sides of the flanges at the top of the inner sills. As they had not been welded yet we used lengths of wood to support both sides of the front bulkhead while working on the doors.*

5 *The outer offside front wing and door and the outer edge of the bulkhead seen from directly above, showing the swage line through the wing and door which should be level so that the open door will not strike the wing. This can be adjusted by easing the wing away from the car slightly on the mounting bolts in the bulkhead. There has to be a fairly large door gap at the front in particular where the door has to clear the front wing and I measured 3/8in (1cm) here*

TR6 RESTORATION

6 *Initially the heelboard was tacked to the rear edge of the propshaft tunnel and its lower flange clamped in alignment with the rear edge of the floor panels.*

7 *The seat pan assembly over the rear axle started life as two parts. The bulging section over the diff. was plug welded in place with the aid of several long welding clamps. Then this assembly was bolted into place and the heelboard was fitted with the flange around its edge wrapping around the seat pan.*

8 *The rear lower panel was installed with our boot floor and floor side assemblies.*

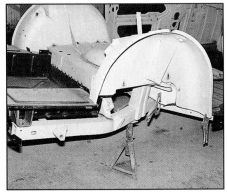

9 *Having achieved satisfactory gaps at the front of the doors we set about fitting the rear wheel arches, which were tack-welded to the edges of the seat pan assembly. Note the new body mounting bracket, at the rear end of the chassis rail, which was made by S.W. Classics.*

10 *Quarter panels were added and spot-welded to the wheel arch flanges.*

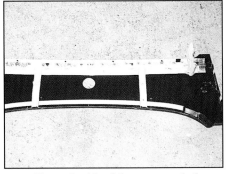

11 *The underside of the new rear deck panel, complete with the stiffeners which were salvaged from the original.*

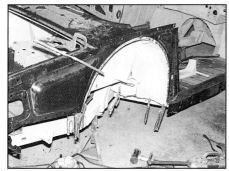

12 *The rear deck panel was clamped into position...*

13 *...then the outer wings and the rear valance assembly were added.*

14 *Having attended to the door gaps and alignments as mentioned in the text, and before installing the 'B' posts, these captive nut assemblies had to be attached to the reproduction rear quarter panels.*

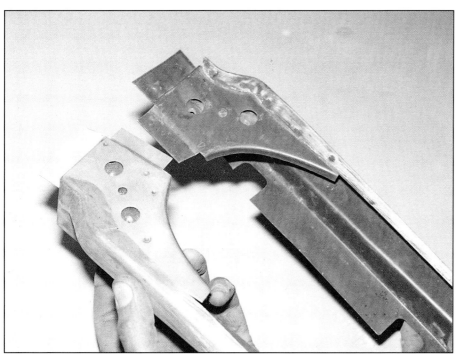

15 *The rear deck side filler panel on the left has been fitted with an S.W. Classics captive nut assembly while the other panel is an original.*

16 *The seatbelt mountings are easily fabricated. They are strong steel brackets folded to match the lower front corner of the rear wheel arches and with a nut welded on.*

17 *The location of one of the seatbelt mountings at the base of the 'B' post/rear wheel arch.*

The companies who have been involved in this TR6 project so far are:
S. W. Classics, Brook House, Dartington, Nr Totnes, Devon. Tel: (0803) 865842.
Machine Mart Limited, 211 Lower Parliament Street, Nottingham NGI 1GN. Tel: (0602) 587666.
Autotrim, Filham Moor Industrial Estate, Ivybridge, Devon. Tel: 0752 893368.
Abbot Blasting of Newton Abbot, Bradley Lane, Newton Abbot. Tel: 68684.
GEM Developments, Beacon Park, Plymouth. Tel: 0752 705989.
J and B. T. Engineering, Unit 3 Brook House, Dartington, Totnes, Devon TQ9 6DJ.
Clive Manvers, Unit 1 Buttons Green Farm, Cockfield, Bury St Edmunds, Suffolk, IP30 OJf. Tel. 0284 828674. Fax: 0284 827063.
Revington TR Spares, Home Farm, Middlezoy, Bridgwater, Somerset, TA7 0PD. Tel: 0823 69437. Fax: 698109.
Rimmer Bros Ltd, Triumph House, Sleaford Road, Bracebridge Heath, Lincoln, LN4 2NA. Tel. 0522 568000, Fax. 0522 567600.
TR Bitz, Lyncastle Way, Barley Castle Trading Estate, Appleton, Warrington, Cheshire, WA4 45T. Tel. 0925 861861, Fax. 0925 860816.
TR GB, 3 Warners Drove, Somersham, Huntingdon, Cambridgeshire PE17 3HW. Tel: 0487 842168. Fax: 740274.

Installing 'B' posts

Then it was necessary to make the door gaps correct between the rear edges of the doors and the rear wings and to get the alignments right along the sides of the car, including the swage lines. When all this has been done the 'B' posts were installed making sure that suitable gaps were maintained between them and the doors.

It is worth delaying repairs to the 'B' posts until this stage is reached so that they can be tried on the car with the doors and sills in place, enabling the correct curvature to be established. To repair them earlier would involve some guesswork, which may well be incorrect.

▶

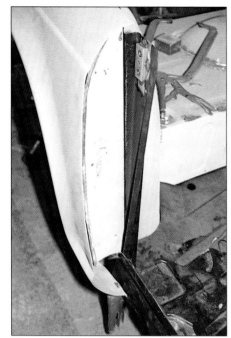

18 *With rear wings and rear deck panel in place we started to trial-fit the rear half of each 'B' post...*

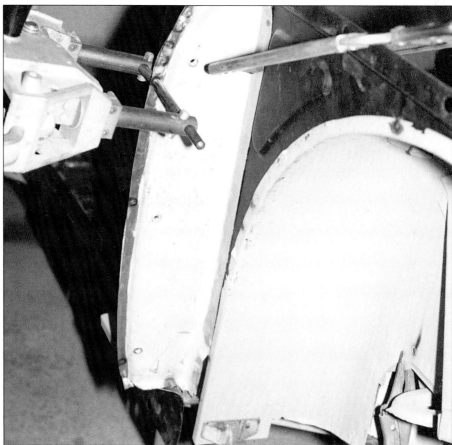

20 *With rear wings and rear deck panel in place we started to trial-fit the rear half of each 'B' post...*

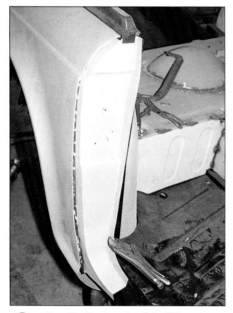

19 *...then the front parts of the 'B' posts and the rear deck side fillers, keeping a close watch throughout on how these additional panels fitted in relation to the doors.*

21 *The upper and lower panels within the rear of the boot were installed...*

22 *...followed by the bootlid. Here again any errors in the gaps and alignments with wings will be visible on the finished car so it is worth spending time getting them right.*

If, as in our car, the rear quarter panels and the rear deck side filler panels are reproductions they need their respective captive nut assemblies fitted (these are available from S.W. Classics). Those on the rear quarter panels really should be fitted before the 'B' posts are installed as it is almost impossible to do so afterwards. New seatbelt mountings were needed too. The bootlid was trial-fitted to see how well it matched up to the rear wings when the appropriate gaps had been achieved.

Then, when satisfied that the whole car was straight, the outer sills (which nearly always need some alterations) went on and the formidable task of welding it all together could begin. However, it should be borne in mind that, so far, all that had been proved was that it was possible to bring the various panels together to make a satisfactory body.

Some dismantling would follow, to create access for the welding, and there was plenty of scope still for things to go wrong, perhaps due to the cumulative effect of several small discrepancies when repositioning panels for welding.

Bracing

Finally, before lifting the bodyshell off the chassis (for painting) the door apertures were braced to prevent distortion of the body. Our bracing pieces were made from folded 16 gauge steel and they remained in place throughout painting and while the body was bolted back on the chassis afterwards.

Had our TR6 included good bulkheads at the beginning of its restoration and, preferably, a chassis which hadn't required quite so much drastic surgery, a very large amount of

time and expense would have been saved. As it was, there was a great deal of trial fitting, dismantling and refitting and further repetition of the same before S.W. Classics brought it all together in time for the Bristol Classic Car Show in March 1991, though it was by no means finished even then.

NEXT MONTH: WORKING ON THE BRAKES AND SUSPENSION.

The principal clubs which specialise in the Triumph TR range are:
The TR Register, 271 High Street, Berkhamstead, Herts, HP4 1AA.
TR Drivers' Club, 39 Brook Street, Benson, Oxon, OX9 6LQ. Tel. 0491 35458.

COTSWOLD VALE
TAYFORTH

Founded in 1970, the TR Register is a flourishing club for enthusiasts and owners of TR2-TR8 and all TR derivatives including Peerless, Warwick GT, Italia and Swallow Doretti.

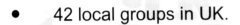

- 42 local groups in UK.

- 20 overseas groups.

- Club regalia sales.

- Full programme of events all year.

- Help with insurance.

- RAC membership discount.

- Race championship.

- Sprint & hillclimb championship.

- Breakdown service.

- Spares discount.

- Technical advice.

- 8 club magazines per year.

New address from 1st November, 1992.
TR Register, 1B Hawksworth, Southmead Industrial Park, Didcot, Oxon OX11 7HR.
Tel: 0235 818866.

TRENT
DORSET
WYDEAN
BRUNEL TRS

CLYDE VALLEY
ABERDEEN

DERBYSHIRE DALES

74

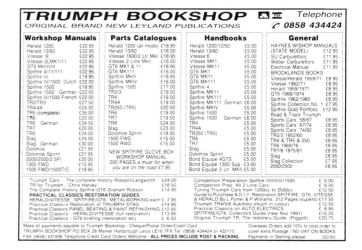
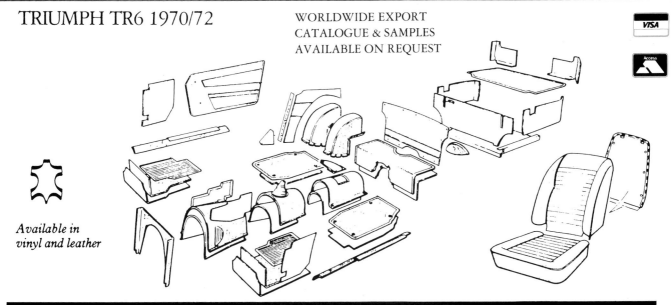

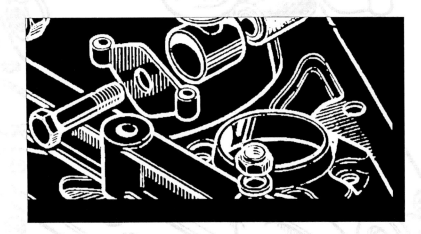
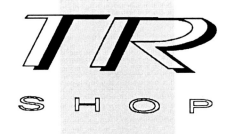

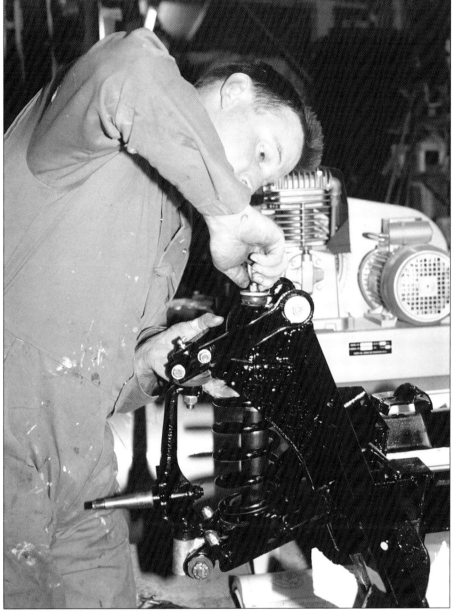

1 *We fitted an Armstrong telescopic damper, attaching the mounting brackets (shown here) to the lower end before passing it through the spring pan and spring. The damper must not be allowed to turn while the top nut is attached and before fitting the locking nut.*

2 *A rubber bush being fitted in a trailing arm. When the bush was about three-quarters of the way in, the trailing arm was tilted in the vice so that the edge of the vice just caught the edge of the arm, allowing space for the bush to be pushed home.*

3 *A trolley jack was used to raise the trailing arm against the spring and, while several of us sat on the chassis to compress the spring sufficiently, the link from the lever arm damper was connected at the rear of the trailing arm with the necessary washers and rubber mountings and a locking nut on the bottom of the link. The lever arm damper bump stops were removed to help this operations but they can be refitted later.*

TR6 RESTORATION

Part 14: John Williams deals with assembling the suspension and steering gear.

By this stage in our TR6 restoration, the pace of work had accelerated somewhat. Previously work had progressed at a steady rate, concentrating on one relatively small part of the car at a time while the rest of the car's parts were well out of the way in the spare parts store, leaving plenty of space for S.W.Classics to get on with other full restorations, plus a multitude of smaller jobs for a never-ending stream of customers.

Now we had reached the point at which there was a bodyshell, plus doors, bonnet and bootlid occupying the paint shop. Various components which would be needed later had been brought to the main workshop for cleaning, overhauling and repainting. In the same workshop the chassis, already repainted, was waiting on stands under a dust sheet for the suspension, brakes and steering components to be fitted and these too had been

laid out in an orderly fashion nearby.

The engine, gearbox and overdrive awaited refitting too and still more equipment had been borrowed from the project's sponsors, Machine Mart, for use when painting the bodyshell. Within a very short time all the major parts of the car would be together again and the slow, careful work of fitting up could carry on for as long as necessary while most of the S.W.Classics personnel caught up with work for other customers.

This month I am going to describe some ▶

Sponsored by

TR6 RESTORATION

aspects of rebuilding the mechanical components on to the chassis but, first, a few notes on rebuilding universal joints.

If the bearings in the rear axle shaft assemblies are worn, Stan Walters (of S.W.Classics) suggests that they should be exchanged for reconditioned assemblies and that the only DIY job on these assemblies is the overhaul of the UJs. Each of the UJs consists of a spider (the cross-shaped part in the centre of the joint) which links two yokes. Each yoke houses a pair of needle-roller bearing assemblies which are held in place by circlips located in grooves. To dismantle a UJ start by loosening the circlips with a punch before removing them with circlip pliers. Then, by using a hammer and drift against one bearing cap, the opposite bearing assembly will be driven out of the yoke. However, rather than hold the yoke (or the shaft) in the vice for this purpose, it is better to support the yoke in a hollow object which is large enough to accommodate the displaced bearing - such as an old socket for example - while using a smaller socket as a drift. This method greatly reduces the risk of distorting the yoke. With one of each pair of bearings driven out of their respective yokes the rest of the assembly should come apart easily.

To reassemble a UJ, put some extra grease into each of the new bearing assemblies but ensure that the rollers remain around the perimeter of the cap. Press a cap into one arm of a yoke, using the vice and making sure that it goes in squarely. Insert the spider while there is sufficient clearance to do so and continue pressing the cap into the yoke until it has cleared the circlip slot.

Fit the circlip. Slide the spider back as necessary until it is protruding from the opposite yoke. Start fitting the second bearing cap by hand (without allowing the bearings to become displaced) then use the vice, and the smaller socket, to press that bearing into the yoke far enough to allow its circlip to be fitted. Use a punch to ensure that the circlips are fully into their grooves and then repeat the procedure on the other yoke. If you meet any significant resistance when pressing the new bearings into place in the vice, stop dismantle and start again. Such resistance may be caused by a roller bearing which has become displaced and to carry on regardless would destroy the whole bearing assembly.

Rear suspension

The pictures show the work in progress on the offside rear suspension. The trailing arm mounting brackets are in pairs and they have notches in their upper edges. The bracket with the three notches fits nearer to the centre of the chassis.

Stan Walters fitted the brackets to the trailing arms away from the chassis, starting by putting the bolts which would go through the chassis rail into the brackets. Then he put the brackets over the bushes in the trailing arms and, prior to fitting each bolt through its bracket and bush, applied some copper grease to the bolt.

The inner bolt was fitted so that its nut was at the end nearest to the centre of the

4 *The inboard part of the driveshaft assembly, which connects to the differential, had this large gaiter fitted to cover its UJ.*

5 *Then the splines on the outer section of the driveshaft assembly were greased and this gaiter was pulled back over them...*

6 *...before the assembly was passed through the trailing arm..*

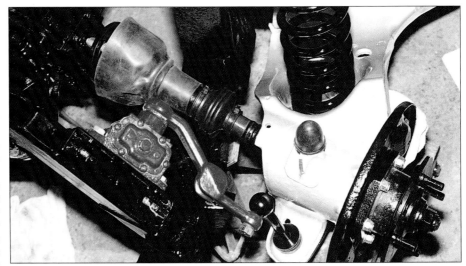

7 *...and the splines on the outer assembly were passed into the inner assembly. The inner end of the small gaiter was fitted round the inner assembly and secured with a clip.*

9 *The upper fulcrum pin should be fitted so that its middle section (which is curved) curves towards the engine. It is possible to fit it the opposite way, so take care.*

10 *Uprated nylon bushes with stainless steel inserts are available but we used standard rubber bushes. A concentrated washing up liquid aids fitting if they're tight..*

chassis. The outer bolt had its nut on the outer end - otherwise, on the finished car, these bolts would be trapped by the chassis and bodywork respectively. Then copper grease was applied to the chassis rail bolts and these were fitted with two shims between each bracket and the chassis. We could not arrive at the correct number of shims at this stage but this will be done later, when the suspension alignment is sorted out.

Front suspension

Next we moved to the nearside front suspension where Stan started by using a 3/8in tap to clean the threads in the top of the turret.

The top front wishbone is stamped 'R' on one side and 'L' on the other side and, when fitting them to the nearside, the 'L' should appear on the upper face. The top rear wishbone is not stamped at all.

Bottom wishbone brackets are all the same and interchangeable. The bushes at the mounting bracket end of the wishbones are pressed into the wishbones using the vice. The bushes at the outer (trunnion end) of the lower wishbones are tapped into the wishbone gently. There is a metal cap followed by a rubber bush which goes round the edge and a metal tube which goes through the whole thing.

Again we fitted a couple of shims behind each of the wishbone/chassis mounting brackets leaving the final adjustment until later. It is permissible to trim a small mount of rubber off the ends of the bushes at the inner ends of the lower wishbones to help insert them into the brackets.

We fitted the rubber oil seal over the threaded section at the bottom of the vertical link then put gear oil into the trunnion before it was threaded on to the link.

Fitting a spring

The next job was to fit the coil spring. For this we used a stout threaded rod with nuts and washers on each end supplemented by a redundant steel pulley at the top and a thick steel bar at the bottom. This amounted to a substitute for Churchill tool number S.112/1.

The spring was placed under the turret (with rubber washers at both ends and the lower spring pan below it) and the threaded rod was passed through the old pulley (laid on top of the turret to spread the load), down through the spring and pan and through the ▶

8 *Old and new vertical links showing corrosion on the old one due to lack of oil. Eventually this can cause the link to snap just above the threaded section.*

11 *It is necessary to fit the brackets to the lower wishbones before fitting the whole assembly to the chassis, otherwise there is insufficient space to fit the wishbone bolts.*

The companies who have been involved in this TR6 project so far are:
S. W. Classics, Brook House, Dartington, Nr Totnes, Devon. Tel: (0803) 865842.
Machine Mart Limited, 211 Lower Parliament Street, Nottingham NGI 1GN. Tel: (0602) 587666.
Autotrim, Filham Moor Industrial Estate, Ivybridge, Devon. Tel: 0752 893368.
Abbot Blasting of Newton Abbot, Bradley Lane, Newton Abbot. Tel: 68684.
GEM Developments, Beacon Park, Plymouth. Tel. 0752 705989.
J and B. T. Engineering, Unit 3 Brook House, Dartington, Totnes, Devon TQ9 6DJ.
Clive Manvers, Unit 1 Buttons Green Farm, Cockfield, Bury St Edmunds, Suffolk, IP30 OJf. Tel. 0284 828674. Fax: 0284 827063.
Revington TR Spares, Home Farm, Middlezoy, Bridgwater, Somerset, TA7 0PD. Tel: 0823 69437. Fax: 698109.
Rimmer Bros Ltd, Triumph House, Sleaford Road, Bracebridge Heath, Lincoln, LN4 2NA. Tel. 0522 568000, Fax. 0522 567600.
TR Bitz, Lyncastle Way, Barley Castle Trading Estate, Appleton, Warrington, Cheshire, WA4 45T. Tel. 0925 861861, Fax. 0925 860816.
TR GB, 3 Warners Drove, Somersham, Huntingdon, Cambridgeshire PE17 3HW. Tel: 0487 842168. Fax: 740274.

12 *When fitting the balljoint assembly between the outer ends of the upper wishbones, note that the inner mounting bolt should be inserted from the front of the assembly and the outer mounting bolt from the rear.*

13 *The very large bolt which goes through the outer ends of the lower wishbones and through the trunnion was smeared with copper grease. This required large washers on both sides of each wishbone and a new splitpin for the slotted nut.*

14 *Plenty of grease was applied to both ends of the steering rack then the two gaiters were fitted. Each of them was secured at both ends by clips.*

15 *The anti-roll bar bracket was fitted to the front lower wishbone on the nearside. Note which way round the bracket fits...*

16 *...then the link assembly was fitted as shown here with a new Nyloc nut.*

TR6 RESTORATION

steel bar which would spread the load under the spring pan. Using this arrangement to hold the spring loosely in place we attached the upper end of the vertical link to the ball joint, leaving the trunnion end unattached for the moment.

Then, gradually, the nuts were tightened on the rod, compressing the spring until it was possible to attach the spring pan loosely to the outer ends of the lower wishbones. This also allowed Stan to fit the trunnion between the wishbones and, eventually, to attach the other wishbone/spring pan nuts and tighten all nuts.

At this point I would like to stress that road springs which have been compressed, even to

a slight extent, are potentially very dangerous. During installation it is essential to watch the spring constantly, ensuring that it is remaining straight while being compressed and that there is no risk of it slipping.

The chassis front extension (whose mounting bolts would be shared later with the front bumper irons) was fitted loosely so that the anti-roll bar mountings could be attached. Rubber bushes had been fitted to the anti-roll bar earlier (with the aid of some Fairy Liquid, which enabled them to slide along the bar). The mounting brackets fitted against these bushes were secured by U-bolts through the chassis front extension.

When the steering rack was mounted on the chassis, two pairs of clamps were used to squeeze the mountings before the nuts were tightened - the object being to achieve a gap of about 1/8in between the movable part of

each mounting and the adjacent flange on the rack. Much later, when the chassis was back on its wheels with the weight of the engine helping to create the necessary clearance, the steering lock stop was fitted at the inboard end of each trunnion. ■

NEXT MONTH: Painting the bodyshell and assembling the brakes.

The principal clubs which specialise in the Triumph TR range are:
The TR Register, 271 High Street, Berkhamstead, Herts, HP4 1AA.
TR Drivers' Club, 39 Brook Street, Benson, Oxon, OX9 6LQ. Tel. 0491 35458.

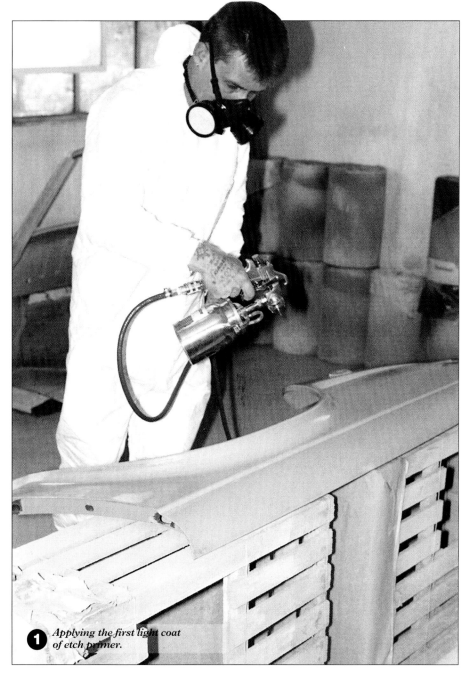

1 *Applying the first light coat of etch primer.*

2 *Wet or dry paper being used wet on a flexible block on a guide-coated panel, the block being moved in different directions to prevent the formation of troughs.*

3 *Here the guide coat has remained in a low area.*

Sponsored by

TR6 RESTORATION

Part 15: Paintwork and brake assembly. John Williams reports.

At last the time had come for S. W. Classics to paint the bodyshell of our TR6. The car was finished in Triumph Sapphire Blue cellulose and this is how it was done:

First, all panels were stripped back to bare metal (which included removing primer from new panels) using a sander with a 40 grit disc and getting into the corners by hand. Next, any dents in the panels were removed by panel beating followed by light filling to eliminate the remaining ripples. Then the panels were blocked using a 3M block fitted with self-adhesive strips of 40 grit paper, finishing with 80 grit to remove the worst of the scratches left by the 40 grit. As this rubbing down was a dry operation it called for the use of dust masks.

Degreasing was the next operation followed by a light coat of etch primer. This coat was given ten minutes to dry before a good coat of etch primer was applied and left for an hour.

Next we used a two-pack high-build primer which makes a hard coating into which there is less sinkage than there would be with cellulose primer. These non-isocyanate primers have three times the build of cellulose primers but they take a little longer to dry than the isocyanate type and the air-fed mask and full safety equipment is not required though a suitable mask should be used when spraying any paint as the work area soon becomes filled with a dense cloud of dry paint dust.

Four coats were applied (giving ample scope for blocking afterwards) and although paint can be put on top after 24 hours, 48 hours would be better.

Back to blocking again now, this time with 600 grit wet or dry on a rubber block and using plenty of water. The awkward bits had to be done by hand of course and it is essential to avoid putting finger marks into the finish. It is advisable to fold up a complete ▶

TR6 RESTORATION

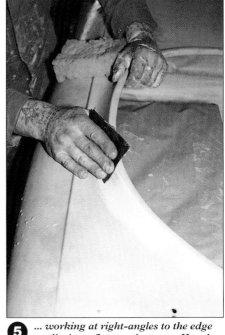

sheet of the paper to make a pad, then hold it in such a way as to keep the fingers flat and, wherever possible, working at right-angles to the direction in which the fingers are pointing.

The objective is to remove all high spots and make a perfect surface before applying the top coats. To this end a guide coat, consisting of 90% thinners and 10% of any dark colour except red, was sprayed lightly over all areas to be blocked. Blocking removed the guide coat from the high areas first and as these areas of primer were reduced in thickness the remaining guide coat in the low areas diminished until it was removed completely.

After blocking, the panels were washed thoroughly, making sure that all sludge was removed from corners etc., then the panels were dried completely. Next they were degreased twice using a degreasing agent applied with a clean, lint-free cloth. Then a tack rag was used to make absolutely sure that no dust was present.

Four coats of cellulose top coat were applied next, each consisting of 50:50 thinners and colour. These were left for a week and then blocked, using 800 wet or dry, dried, degreased and tacked before another four coats were applied and left for a further week. This time 1000 wet or dry was used for blocking and the finish was dried, degreased and tacked as usual ready for the final four coats. The last two coats could be thinned down to 75% thinners - this helps to "flow" the paint a bit better and make it a bit flatter. The final coats were left for a week.

Now the paint was blocked using fine wet or dry. This is a buff coloured paper made by 3M which comes in half-quire sizes and is marked 'F' on the reverse side. Soap and water was used at this stage, plenty of soap in fact. When a matt finish had been achieved the surface was washed thoroughly to remove all traces of soap and the panels were dried.

Now it was time to use T-cut, working a square foot at a time and "T- cutting" each square foot perhaps three times until it had a glass finish. Care has to be taken to avoid rubbing through the paint on edges and swage lines at this stage though the risk of doing so on our car was small as there was a lot of paint on it by now. All that remained then was to apply a good wax polish.

The bodyshell of our TR6 was painted inside and underneath and the doors, wings, bonnet and bootlid were painted separately. After the first four topcoats had been appled to everything, the wings were bolted on the body and the remaining topcoats were applied with these in place. The doors, bonnet and bootlid remained separate from the main part of the body until they had been

4 *Here Andy is flatting the upper section of a wing where it curves round to its top edge, moving the block parallel to the top edge of the wing at first. He will finish by...*

5 *... working at right-angles to the edge to eliminate flats on the curve. Here he is flatting the edges with care to avoid rubbing through the primer.*

8 *Twelve top coats were applied in groups of four at weekly intervals with hours of tedious but vital flatting in between plus T-cutting and polishing afterwards.*

9 *Left to right: The DeVilbiss JGA, Binks 222 and Clarke Air Super Pro guns. All three produced good results. Replacement parts are readily available .*

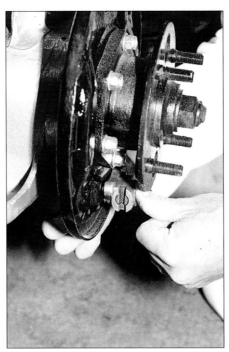

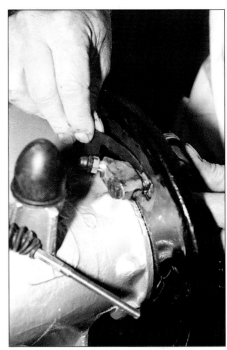

12 *First the brake adjuster unit was fitted as shown here, then the wheel cylinder in the top of the backplate with a smear of copper grease to help it slide against the backplate.*

13 *Next, Stan fitted the locking plate retaining spring, sliding it into place from the front...*

6 *Degreasing prior to using the tack rag before applying the first of the top coats*

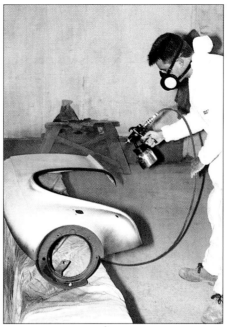

7 *The top coats were sprayed on to all the edges of the panel before covering the other areas.*

10 *The Airmaster Tiger 10/60 compressor rated at 9cfm and fitted with a 50 litre receiver. It coped well with a 'professional spray gun.*

11 *The Airmaster AM 15EF150 delivers 14cfm and has a 150 litre receiver. This and the Tiger were used at 65psi delivery pressure.*

14 *...then the distance washer, also from the front, then the wheel cylinder locking plate (Picture 15), which was fed between...*

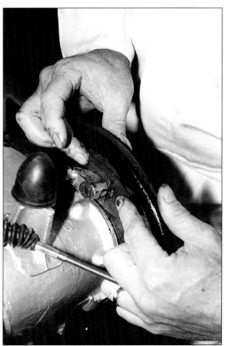

15 *... the other two parts from the rear. It is worth applying copper grease to these parts before the rubber dust cover goes over the lever and around the edge of the retainers.*

painted completely.

A stonechip paint (over primer) was used under the wheelarches and on the underside of the body. This is a rubberised, cellulose-based compound which was spread on using a Schutz gun and then body colour paint was applied on top.

Compressors and guns

While painting the TR6 we tried out two more compressors and three sprayguns from the project's sponsors, Machine Mart. The compressors were an Airmaster Tiger 10/60 (rated at 9cfm) and an Airmaster AM 15EF150 (14 cfm) with 50 and 150 litre tanks respectively.

The sprayguns were a DeVilbiss JGA (requiring 10 cfm at 50psi or 14 cfm at 70psi) which is a very popular gun with the professionals, a Binks 222 (6 cfm at 50psi) which is also well regarded and a Clarke Air Super Pro (11 cfm average) which was new to the market at the time but was believed to be on a par with the Binks. My main concern was to discover which of the guns, if any, would not work satisfactorily with the Tiger 10/60 compressor. If all three worked I anticipated that all three would produce a good result, as indeed they did. However, in theory at least, the DeVilbiss should not have worked for very long with the Tiger 10/60 before running out of air and, I wondered whether the Clarke gun would have the same problem.

A major advantage of a compressor which incorporates a decent tank (or air receiver, to use the correct term) is that there is a sufficient reserve of compressed air, at a pressure higher than the delivery pressure, to enable the spraygun (or other air tool) to run for longer than it would if it relied on the actual output of the compressor alone.

On both compressors the delivery pressure was set at 65psi to allow for some fall in pressure caused by long air lines. Andy Jackson, the painter at S.W. Classics, pressed on at quite a pace, measuring and mixing, spraying, swapping compressors and cleaning and swapping guns. The latter entails dismantling the gun and washing the individual parts in gun wash and then reassembling it and spraying gun wash through it to wash out the nozzles.

Andy finished two days of this activity by applying a coat of colour to three TR6 wings in succession, using the DeVilbiss connected to the Tiger 10/60. We were pleasantly surprised at how well this combination of compressor and gun had performed. Then, someone (no names mentioned) who thought that the larger compressor was being used admitted that he had turned off the Tiger 10/60 as Andy finished the first wing. Somehow this seemed a fitting ending to a frantic couple of days but it did prove the ▶

The principal clubs which specialise in the Triumph TR range are:
The TR Register, 271 High Street, Berkhamstead, Herts, HP4 1AA.
TR Drivers' Club, 39 Brook Street, Benson, Oxon, OX9 6LQ. Tel. 0491 35458.

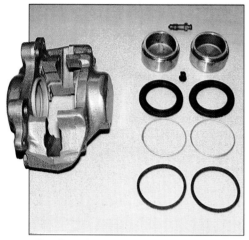

16 *One of the calipers cleaned and painted, with the new parts ready for fitting.*

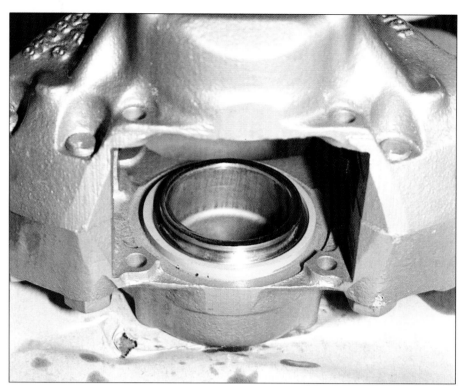

18 *With the piston in this position its own seal fits partly around the groove around the piston and partly over the edge of the cylinder.*

17 *The piston had to be inserted into the cylinder, care being taken not to damage the ring.*

19 *A wire ring then fits around the edge of the seal and though I could see no convincing reason why it should stay put, apparently it will do so.*

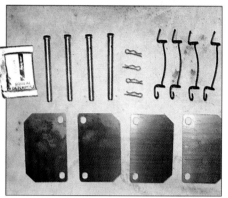

20 *The later calipers have 3/16in brake pad retaining pins and the earlier ones have thicker pins. The fitting kit includes anti-rattle springs.*

important point that the top quality DeVilbiss spraygun would work quite happily with the Tiger 10/60 compressor, even though this seemed extremely unlikely on paper.

Brakes

Finally, I would like to continue from where I left off last month with a few notes on assembling the brakes. The brake backplates are not interchangeable - you must fit the correct one to each side of the car. The pictures show the order in which the wheel cylinder retaining spring, locking plate and distance washer were fitted to the offside rear brake assembly.

Stan joined the brake shoes by their top spring and then fitted them around the wheel cylinder (into the slot at the rear side of the cylinder and around the lever at the front of the cylinder). The bottom spring was inserted afterwards and then the shoes were pulled around both sides of the adjuster, followed by the shoe retainers, one for each shoe. Finally the brake drum was fitted, tapping it with a soft mallet if necessary and securing it with two screws.

The first job here was to make sure that the groove in the caliper was clean before inserting the sealing ring. We were using silicone brake fluid and everything was liberally dosed with it.

Squeal deterrent was smeared on the backs of the pads and on both sides of the shims which fit between the pads and the pistons. The torque setting for the brake caliper mounting bolts is 65lb/ft.

NEXT MONTH: BUILDING A DOOR, AND SOME WIRING AND FITTING UP. ∎

The companies who have been involved in this TR6 project so far are:
S. W. Classics, Brook House, Dartington, Nr Totnes, Devon. Tel: (0803) 865842.
Machine Mart Limited, 211 Lower Parliament Street, Nottingham NGI 1GN. Tel: (0602) 587666.
Autotrim, Filham Moor Industrial Estate, Ivybridge, Devon. Tel: 0752 893368.
Abbot Blasting of Newton Abbot, Bradley Lane, Newton Abbot. Tel: 68684.
GEM Developments, Beacon Park, Plymouth. Tel. 0752 705989.
J and B. T. Engineering, Unit 3 Brook House, Dartington, Totnes, Devon TQ9 6DJ.
Clive Manvers, Unit 1 Buttons Green Farm, Cockfield, Bury St Edmunds, Suffolk, IP30 OJf. Tel. 0284 828674. Fax: 0284 827063.
Revington TR Spares, Home Farm, Middlezoy, Bridgwater, Somerset, TA7 0PD. Tel: 0823 69437. Fax: 698109.
Rimmer Bros Ltd, Triumph House, Sleaford Road, Bracebridge Heath, Lincoln, LN4 2NA. Tel. 0522 568000, Fax. 0522 567600.
TR Bitz, Lyncastle Way, Barley Castle Trading Estate, Appleton, Warrington, Cheshire, WA4 45T. Tel. 0925 861861, Fax. 0925 860816.
TR GB, 3 Warners Drove, Somersham, Huntingdon, Cambridgeshire PE17 3HW. Tel: 0487 842168. Fax: 740274.

TR6 RESTORATION

Part 16: John Williams oversees the rebuilding of a door and a seat cushion.

Many owners seem reluctant to tackle the sometimes fiddly work on the interior of a door, but if access is good, as on the TR6, it can be simple. **But be careful to avoid dropping anything inside the door, which could cause a small dent in the doorskin.**

The first job was to fit the front vertical glass channel which was secured by two bolts through the sloping, forward facing section at the upper front corner of the door and by a third bolt at the bottom. Next the window regulator assembly was inserted and attached to the door by three bolts in a triangular pattern more or less in the middle of the door and four more in the vicinity of the winding mechanism.

The bottom window stop, complete with the glass channel bottom tie rod was fitted next. The tie rod is simply a length of stout wire which hooks around the lower end of each glass channel - the rear end of it remained loose for the time being as the rear glass channel had yet to be fitted. The glass stop, a simple right-angle bracket, was secured by two small bolts in the middle of the door near the bottom.

It may be necessary to remove some of the

① *The remote control assembly being fitted. This need not be done until just before the door trim panel is replaced.*

paint from the hole for the door lock so that the private lock (the part operated by the key) will fit. Strictly speaking the lock should fit as indicated in the picture caption. This is by pushing it through from the outside of the door, the right way up of course with its lever pointing towards the rear of the door, until both sprung legs on the built-in clip jump outwards behind the skin of the door to hold the lock in place.

That's fine in theory, but with a lot of paint on a newly restored door the lock may not push into the door far enough to release the spring clip. There are two ways to solve this ▶

Sponsored by

2 *Two sets of bolts which secure the window winding mechanism, also (bottom right) the third bolt for the front glass channel.*

TR6 RESTORATION

problem. The first is to shorten the legs of the spring clip until they fit - which is a bit "trial and error" with the risk of overdoing it. Alternatively, remove the clip from the lock, fit the lock, then attach the clip to the lock inside the door - which is a bit of a fiddle but it can be done.

The lock mechanism, which fits inside the rear of the door, is the same as that used on the Mk III Spitfire (as is the striker on the B post) but at first we thought that we were mistaken about this. The problem was that the lever failed to reach the push-button assembly in the door handle. We didn't spot the reason for this right away but sent the lock to the welding shop where John Holmes added some metal to the upper lever. TR6 locks are not available new at the time of writing and £25 is being asked for secondhand ones. Mk III Spitfire locks are not available new either, but it shouldn't be hard to find secondhand ones at £5-£10 each. With its modified lever the lock worked perfectly - then we spotted the cause of the problem.

The door handle on the nearside door was almost five millimetres forward of where it should have been in relation to the private lock, when compared with the same components on the offside door, though both private locks were exactly the same distance from the rear edges of their respective doors. Clearly the new nearside doorskin had been supplied with the door handle's bolt holes in the wrong places - a discrepancy which would not have been noticed without the aid of a tape measure.

The order of assembly at this stage is worth noting: The locking mechanism has to be installed in the door before the rear glass channel. Several trim clips have to be attached to the flanges of the window slot in the door and the rearmost of these (together with the rear ends of the inner and outer weatherstrips) should be fitted before the rear glass channel is installed. Then we fitted the remote control assembly though this could have waited until later. Then the glass itself

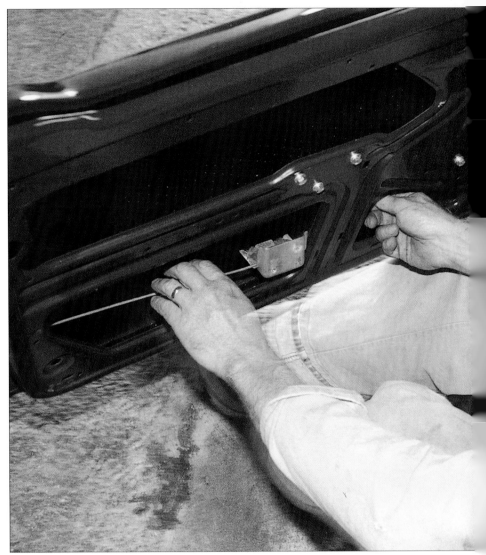

3 *Here the bottom glass stop assembly is going in - eventually its ends would hook around the backs of both glass channels.*

4 *The lock fits by pushing it through from the outside of the door until the spring clip engages behind the doorskin.*

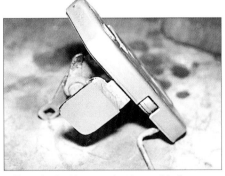

5 *The locking mechanism with the enlarged upper lever - a simple modification for a welder.*

6 *The locking mechanism has to be installed in the door before the rear glass channel.*

7 *How the remote control assembly connects to the lock - difficult to photograph once inside the door.*

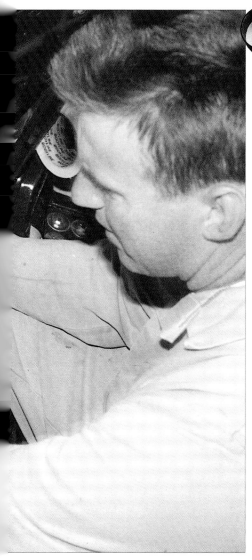

8 *The tool on the hooked end of which each trim clip was lowered through the slot then pulled up on the flange.*

9 *The upper glass stop bracket (right-hand door) - not illustrated in my copy of the parts manual.*

was installed before the rest of the clips (which could have scratched the glass). We used the simple "home-made" tool shown in the picture to lower each of these clips into the slot and then pull them up on to the flange.

Earlier the new window glass had its glazing channel and metal channel attached together with the weather curtain. The latter was made from the heavy polythene in which the glass was wrapped when delivered. This whole assembly was lowered through the slot in the top of the door until there was suffi-

cient space to fit the remaining trim clips.

Once the clips were in, the weatherseals simply pushed down on to them. Then the glass was lifted high (a helper was needed at this stage to hold the glass for a few moments), the winder mechanism was raised and unbolted and its runners were slotted into the channels at the bottom of the glass before it was bolted to the door again.

The upper glass stop bracket is slightly contoured to match the inner door panel to which it is bolted through two slotted holes just to the rear of the remote control mechanism. These brackets are not interchangeable between the doors and they limit the movement of one of the rails of the window regulator assembly. The upper glass stop was fitted next but its final adjustment had to wait for the new hood to be installed.

All that remained was to mask off the three lower apertures in the inner face of the door, to protect the back of the trim panel from moisture, then the trim panel and door handles were fitted.

Incidentally, a Tex Universal Door Mirror was fitted to the driver's door. This chrome plated mirror (SRHF1, part number H68990) came complete with fittings including the plastic mounting pad for the outer surface of the door.

Fitting up

Before I launch into interior trim work I must mention the rewiring and the enormous amount of fitting up which was done by Stan Walters at S.W. Classics. As Stan pointed out, it is vital to use grommets everywhere that the wiring passes through body panels and equally good practice to line the loom

supporting tabs on the body with a new plastic sleeve. It must be a sign of the times that every single grommet in a batch supplied by a well-known Triumph supplier was labelled 'Made in Taiwan'.

When installing all the items which go under the dashboard on the bulkhead, start with those nearest to the bulkhead so that your efforts will not be obstructed later. Quite a few parts installed early in the fitting up stage are not necessarily in exactly their final positions, particularly where the position depends on control cables, hoses etc. Minor adjustments can be made later.

It is worth fitting new wheelboxes for the wipers when restoring one of these cars because it is practically impossible to get at them once the car is all built up again - a fact that caused us much grief when fitting the racks later, when we discovered slight constrictions in the pipework which was practically inaccessible.

The driver's seat

Interior trim work on our TR6 was carried out by Autotrim, of Filham Moor Industrial Estate, Ivybridge, Devon, (Tel 0752 893368). This included making and fitting the new carpets and hood and the first job was to ▶

The companies who have been involved in this TR6 project so far are:
S. W. Classics, Brook House, Dartington, Nr Totnes, Devon. Tel: (0803) 865842.
Machine Mart Limited, 211 Lower Parliament Street, Nottingham NGI 1GN. Tel: (0602) 587666.
Autotrim, Filham Moor Industrial Estate, Ivybridge, Devon. Tel: 0752 893368.
Abbot Blasting of Newton Abbot, Bradley Lane, Newton Abbot. Tel: 68684.
GEM Developments, Beacon Park, Plymouth. Tel. 0752 705989.
J and B. T. Engineering, Unit 3 Brook House, Dartington, Totnes, Devon TQ9 6DJ.
Clive Manvers, Unit 1 Buttons Green Farm, Cockfield, Bury St Edmunds, Suffolk, IP30 OJf. Tel. 0284 828674. Fax: 0284 827063.
Revington TR Spares, Home Farm, Middlezoy, Bridgwater, Somerset, TA7 0PD. Tel: 0823 69437. Fax: 698109.
Rimmer Bros Ltd, Triumph House, Sleaford Road, Bracebridge Heath, Lincoln, LN4 2NA. Tel. 0522 568000, Fax. 0522 567600.
TR Bitz, Lyncastle Way, Barley Castle Trading Estate, Appleton, Warrington, Cheshire, WA4 45T. Tel. 0925 861861, Fax. 0925 860816.
TR GB, 3 Warners Drove, Somersham, Huntingdon, Cambridgeshire PE17 3HW. Tel: 0487 842168. Fax: 740274.

10 *This was as far as the dismantling of our seat back needed to go. A new cushion diaphragm was fitted.*

11 *The (relatively) easy way to manoeuvre diaphragm hooks into the holes in the frame using a loop of string.*

12 *The underside of the new cushion cover showing the three flaps of material for glueing to the foam.*

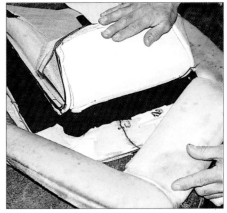

13 *Here the flaps have been glued to the lower foam, more glue was added and the shaped foam is being positioned.*

14 *The foam/hessian skirt being glued on, to soften the sides of the seat frame before the cover is fitted.*

15 *The cushion cover was turned inside-out so that the front and sides were rolled rather than pulled into place.*

16 *A fair amount of stretching and shoving is always needed to produce a good, smooth finish free of ripples.*

TR6 RESTORATION

rebuild the driver's seat. Autotrim's proprietor, Ian Roper, made it look easy.

If you are going to rebuild your own seats start by dismantling just one of them (keeping the other intact for reference) and do this with great care to avoid destroying anything which might be re-usable or which will be needed for use as a pattern. Despite the dreadful state of the TR6 at the beginning of this restoration the driver's seat was in quite a good condition. However, rubber cushions become quite delicate with age and are easily torn, yet if they remain intact their useful life can be greatly extended by the addition of extra padding or reinforcement. It is not a total disaster if the foam disintegrates because it can be replaced - but it all adds to the cost of the job.

The seat cushion comprised a rubber diaphragm attached by double-ended hooks to the metal frame on all four sides. Over the diaphragm was a layer of hessian and on top of this a flat layer of foam rubber about 1/2in thick. Three pieces of shaped rubber foam formed the raised edges of the cushion and a skirt of thin foam extended from the rear

corner of the cushion on one side to the rear corner on the other side and the cover was stretched over all of this and then glued and clipped to the frame on all four sides, the clips being either flat or round to suit the part of the frame to which they fit. If you rebuild your own seat you will want to save as many of the clips as possible and note where they should be used.

Ian replaced the hessian and, using an ozone-friendly aerosol spray-on upholstery adhesive, attached some thin new foam to the shaped pieces for the edges of the cushion. Then he made the new vinyl cover in four parts. The first of these was the central part which extends from the seat frame at the rear to the piping at the front edge and all of it, except for the single layer of vinyl at the rear which stretches around the seat frame, comprised three layers of material - the vinyl, the base material and a thin layer of foam in between. Parallel lines of stitches across this section produced the fluted effect and about 3/4in. of spare material was left on the side and front edges so that they could be sewn to the adjacent panels.

The side panels were cut out next, again a little oversize. Then these were sewn to the central section with new piping sandwiched in between to complete the upper surface of the cushion cover. Then the outer skirt, a single piece of vinyl, was sewn on, again with piping.

Extra flaps of material were sewn to the underside of the cushion cover around the edges of the fluted area (as shown in the pic-

tures) and these were glued to the flat layer of foam referred to earlier. Then the shaped pieces of rubber were glued in place. A new skirt was made in one piece for the front and sides of the seat and then glued in place around the edge of the frame. This comprised a strip of thin foam to which was glued some hessian (to protect the foam from the metal frame). Prior to fitting the seat cushion cover Ian applied glue to the base of the cushion (the hessian), around the edge of the metal frame and on the diaphragm itself so that the whole structure wouldn't move about. Having fitted the cover, with all the little adjustments which are always necessary to get the final shape right, Ian attached the edges to the seat frame with the appropriate spring clips, pulling the cover tight as he did so. Excess material was then trimmed off the edges underneath the seat. ∎

NEXT MONTH: FINISHING THE SEAT AND INSTALLING THE HOOD AND CARPETS.

The workshop at Autotrim while hood and carpet work was in progress.

2 The rear of the seat back with hardboard panel and cover removed, showing Pirelli webbing and wire supports.

3 Thin sheets of lined foam were glued to the existing foam sections at the sides of the seat back.

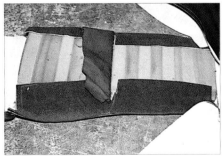

4 The original blocks of foam were transferred to the new cover and the long narrow edges glued around the foam.

TR6 RESTORATION

Part 16: John Williams oversees work on a seat and fitting the hood and carpet as work on the car nears completion.

It's back to Autotrim at Ivybridge, Devon (telephone 0752 893368) this month to see how Ian Roper finished off the seat which we started last month and how he fitted the hood while Nick Johns made and fitted the carpets.

The hardboard panel at the back of the seat, which was attached to the frame by several spring clips, was removed followed by the cover. Then the centre section of the seat, consisting of the fluted vinyl cover and the foam filling, was taken out in one piece leaving the Pirelli webbing in place together with the foam pads up the sides of the seat back and across the top. TR6 seats came in

different styles at different times and for different markets but all had wire seat squab supports (in the seat back). Replacements for these wire supports are unobtainable so if they cannot be re-used some improvisation becomes necessary. Fortunately these were in good condition on our seat, as was the Pirelli webbing.

Ian started by reinforcing the remaining foam on the seat back with an additional layer of thin, lined foam. Then he made the new cover using the original to provide patterns. The foam blocks were transferred from the old central section of the cover to the new one (also necessary when using ready-made

5 *The sides of the back cover in position - one here already has tabs to feed between the webbing.*

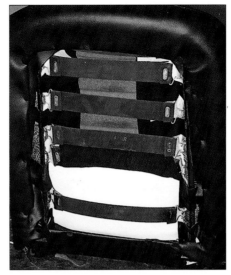

6 *A cloth flap at the rear of the centre panel should be glued around one of the webbings.*

7 *Note the piping on the outer and lower edges of the seat back cover and the shape of the centre section.*

10 *The rear hood rail was glued into a flap under the hood through which it was bolted to the rear deck.*

11 *Seven press studs for the tonneau cover were pop-riveted to the rear edge of the hood.*

TR6
RESTORATION

The principal clubs which specialise in the Triumph TR range are:
The TR Register, 271 High Street, Berkhamstead, Herts, HP4 1AA.
TR Drivers' Club, 39 Brook Street, Benson, Oxon, OX9 6LQ. Tel. 0491 35458.

covers) which was fluted and had piping attached to its right and left edges and a cloth flap at the rear which, when glued around one of the pieces of Pirelli webbing, formed the shape of the central panel about half-way down the seat.

The rest of the seat back cover was made as a separate item using one piece of vinyl for the top, back and sides and two further pieces for the front panels. Then a small piece of vinyl was added to the bottom edge of each of the front panels to tuck underneath the bottom of the foam on each side and a further piece of vinyl was added under the bottom edges of the sides of the cover to form pockets.

There are pieces of hardboard with built-in brackets which attached to the seat frame and, when these are placed in the pockets they support the sides of the seat and form the correct shape.

Making the hood

The hood was made of Everflex by Ian Roper at Autotrim, starting at the back and building it in four sections, each of which bridged the gaps between hood frame rails and hood-sticks. The reconditioned hood frame was on the car already and this was used for reference and trial fittings.

I am not going to describe the hood making operation in detail here but I think it worth mentioning how a window panel was installed. The rearmost section of the hood started off as a double layer of Everflex, these

layers being sewn together along a line which marked the maximum size of the window panel plus a couple of millimetres all round.

Then, from the upper layer of Everflex (which will be the outside layer of the hood), Ian cut out an area which was about 1.5cm smaller than the finished window all round, leaving the lower layer of Everflex intact to protect the window material from scratching while it was being moved about on the bench or trial fitted on the car.

Next the window material was cut out to fit and positioned with its edges sandwiched between the upper and lower layers of hood material. The next stage was to cut the corners of the window aperture on the outer layer of Everflex sufficiently to allow the edges of the material all round the window to be folded under.

Then a line of stitches was placed very close to the edge of the Everflex all round the window, ie. through the (now) double upper layer of Everflex, the transparent window material and the single lower layer of Everflex. Finally, when the hood fitting had been completed, the inner layer of Everflex was cut out close to that line of stitches leaving a very neat finish all around the window. The same method was used on all three windows in the hood.

Whether making a hood in this way or simply fitting a ready-made hood the hood frame needs to be erected and fitted with two lengths of webbing. The webbing should extend from the header rail (above the wind-screen) over the three hoodsticks to the rearmost rail which attaches to the rear deck. The rear end of each piece of webbing has to be made into a loop which passes through a slot in the rear rail and is prevented from escaping from the slot by a short wire rod through the hoop beneath the rail.

With the three hoodsticks positioned correctly, the webbing was pop-riveted to each of them, sandwiching the webbing between either the original webbing securing plates or rivet washers and the hoodsticks. To prevent damage to the hood from plates, washers or rivets any sharp edges or corners should be hammered down to follow the contours of the hoodsticks and it is worth glueing a small piece of webbing over the top of the metal parts for added protection.

8 *The three seams across the top of the hood were welded rather than sewn - to make them weatherproof.*

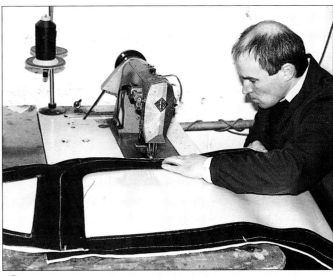

9 *Sewing the rear hood panel with the inner layer of Everflex still in place to protect the windows.*

The forward hoodstick, and the one above the rear window, had several press studs pop-rivetted to them on which to secure flaps which were incorporated in the hood - thus preventing the hood from lifting excessively during fast driving.

The first job on the actual hood was to place it over the frame, position it as accurately as possible and mark the centre of the hood under the flap at the rear - there is a stud hole in the centre of the rearmost rail. The rearmost rail was then glued into the flap under the rear edge of the hood (using Dunlop S1358 adhesive) and studs were fitted to the outside face of the hood at the lower rear to take the tonneau cover.

The hinged upper side rails of the hood above the door glass have Velcro on them, as has the hood which wraps around. Channels for the window seals were attached to the underside of those rails by means of small nuts and bolts. The channels can be adjusted to align with the glass.

With the pins in place in the webbing loops the rear rail was bolted into place on the body with the hood resting on the bootlid. The next stage was to apply adhesive to the front rail of the hood frame above the windscreen. By this time Ian had had the workshop heater turned on for some time as the hood was more pliable and easier to manipulate when warm. The rear end was straightened and the rear rail tightened down on to the body.

Then the front rail was secured to the top of the windscreen frame and the hood itself was pulled tightly over that rail to produce a neat appearance across the rest of the upper frame. The hood remained attached to the front rail now (on account of the glue applied earlier).

When Ian was satisfied with the way the hood fitted in the vicinity of the rear quarterlights the positions of the studs, already on the body, were marked with chinagraph pencil on the hood, holes were punched and the other halves of the press stud assemblies were attached to the hood.

The whole of the lower rear edge of the hood was then fastened down to the body from door to door. Then a line was made on the outer surface of the hood with a chinagraph pencil to mark the front edge of the front rail. The front rail was released from the

12 *Ian fastens the press studs below the quarterlights while Nick Johns works on the interior.*

13 *The leading edge of the front rail was marked on the hood using a chinagraph pencil.*

15 *The door window seals were fitted later after the channels were adjusted to suit the glass.*

14 *Then the channel was fitted to the front rail, over the Everflex, followed by the rubber seal.*

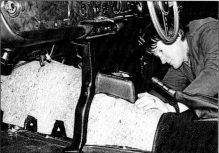

16 *The felt in two pieces on the tunnel with the bracket assembly temporarily in place.*

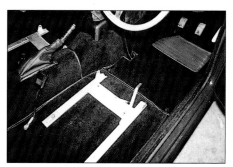

17 *The floor carpet sections simply overlapped the edges of the tunnel carpet.*

windscreen frame, about an inch of hood material was glued to the underside of the rail and the surplus was trimmed off. A channel was rivetted to the rail (over the hood material) and the surplus Everflex behind the channel was trimmed off before the rubber seal was fitted in the channel.

Obviously one of the objectives, when fitting a hood, is to eliminate ripples in the hood material and in the window panels as far as possible. However, it is worth bearing in mind that a hood which is really tight in the warm workshop will become a great deal tighter in a colder situation putting an immense strain on seams etc. and certainly shortening its life.

Some slight ripples, particularly in the window panels and surrounding hood material, should disappear within days of the hood being fitted as the stresses within the hood settle down under the influence of temperature fluctuations.

While Ian Roper was making and fitting the hood at Autotrim, Nick Johns was making and fitting the carpets. Nick's first job was to fit the reproduction glass fibre gearbox/overdrive cover. Though it would be naive to expect any replacement panel, reproduction or otherwise, to fit perfectly at the first attempt, this cover was too long from front to rear, not deep enough (especially in its rear 4-5in) and it was the wrong shape on the offside edge where it should meet the floor. The bulge above the speedometer drive was not large enough, and had to be removed and modified and the hole for the gearlever's

rubber boot was too small. Apart from all that it was perfect!

The gearbox cover had an overlay of thick felt. This was made in two sections which met under the bracket assembly, the rear section being long enough to pass under the edge of the carpet around the handbrake lever. The felt was glued to hold it temporarily while the carpet was fitted and then cut-outs were made around the carpet fasteners on the gearbox cover.

Carpet for the gearbox cover and transmission tunnel was made in three sections. The two forward sections, which met under the

bracket assembly, had the thick felt underneath them. The rear section, which incorporated a gaiter for the handbrake, had a thin foam glued and stitched to it.

The floor carpet was made in four sections and, although very good quality carpet was used, foam was glued and stitched to the underside before the binding was stitched to the edges. This added substantially to the "depth" of the carpet and to insulation and soundproofing.

NEXT MONTH: THE FINAL EPISODE - COUNTING THE COST.

TR6 RESTORATION

Part 17: Concluding the series and counting the cost of returning our project car to 'new' condition. Report by John Williams.

The end of this series has arrived all too quickly. All that remains for me to do is to itemise the costs involved in this project and draw some conclusions. The finished car, which was displayed at the Bristol Classic Car Show, has been described as magnificent. So it should be. The restorers, S.W. Classics take immense pride in their work and this has been fully justified once again.

This has been a very expensive restoration and the main reason has been that, in the best traditions of *Practical Classics* projects, we started with a particularly poor example of a TR6. Therefore, not only did chassis members and body panels account for £2,687 (excluding VAT) but we had to spend almost the same again on the interior and the hood, and almost £1,000 on electrical items. No wonder that the project cost well over £18,000 in labour alone, despite S.W. Classics' very reasonable hourly rate of £13.50. A private owner could have saved quite a lot of money by starting with a better car and carrying out some of the work at home.

It's easy to make trite comments about how a better car at the outset would have saved money but the truth of this came home to me

● *On the road, with the Editor at the wheel. The car really does drive as well as it looks - it's a real pain having to stick to running-in speeds!*

quite forcefully when I was typing out the very long and detailed list of costs which is included here. What could I leave out to save space? Well, at first I thought that I would list all the items which had cost, say, £50 or more. Surely they would account for most of the expense and the total of the remaining small items would be such that I could list it as 'Miscellaneous'?

This approach simply wouldn't work. Those little items added up to an enormous amount of money. To give you a realistic idea of costs, which could be applied, for example, to a

Sponsored by

TR6
RESTORATION

● *Where it started - a derelict TR6 with only a few mechanical spares worth salvaging.*

● *S.W. Classics saved these body panels but every one of them needed a lot of work.*

Principal clubs which specialise in the Triumph TR range are:
The TR Register, 271 High Street, Berkhamsted, Herts, HP4 1AA. Tel: 0442 865906.
TR Drivers' Club, 39 Brook Street, Benson, Oxon, OX9 6LQ. Tel. 0491 35458.

partial or complete TR6 restoration which has yet to be started, I settled for the list shown here which has been condensed somewhat but from which nothing has been deleted. Please note that the figures are rounded to the nearest pound and that items which are listed together here are not necessarily supplied together.

The equipment supplied by the the project's sponsors, Machine Mart, was put to good use by S.W. Classics, not just on this restoration but on other work in hand during the past 18 months or so, and most of the equipment was purchased by S.W. Classics at the end of the project and is working there still. In the summary which follows, prices are quoted to the nearest pound and include VAT but not delivery.

The Clarkeweld 120E MIG welder (£200) could not be faulted but it was let down by the small gas bottles supplied with it. There are gas-flow problems associated with these bottles once they are part used and they are, in any case, an expensive way to buy gas. Obviously this criticism applies equally to other MIG welders and to other brands of MIGs and anyone who anticipates carrying out a lot of welding would be well advised to obtain a large bottle adapter and arrange to obtain the gas supply from a local source. Adapters are available from Machine Mart for use with an Argon/CO_2 mixture or CO_2 on its own.

My previous experience of spot welders,

● *What a contrast with the "before" picture! Those front side/direction indicatior lamps cost an amazing £90 each - and the rechromed bumper was £220.*

● *From the rear. Our TR6 is the faster and consequently more desirable 150bhp version - post-1973 models were detuned to improve economy.*

CHASSIS/BODY PANELS	(£2,687)
1 pr rear legs under boot floor	£40
1 pr (trailing arm) chassis legs	£50
1 pr chassis side members	£150
1 pr front turret to chassis supports	£36
1 rear diff. bridge	£60
2 floors	£120
2 inner sills	£24
2 outer sills	£45
4 sill end caps	£20
1 pr B-post backs	£30
4 floor to chassis brackets	£32
4 outer wings	£480
4 inner wings	£260
4 wing fitting kits/2 front baffle plates	£44
1 bonnet	£250
1 bootlid	£130
1 front panel	£149
2 door skins	£100
1 pr front bulkhead front panels	£54
1 pr front bulkhead to arch supports	£36
1 pr front bulkhead vertical supports	£18
2 front bulkhead sides	£50
1 rear upright kick panel	£27
1 rear bulkhead floor section	£65
2 rear bulkhead floor brackets	£15
1 boot floor and side panels	£110
1 pr boot floor to chassis mounts	£50
1 rear deck	£50
1 pr tonneau sides	£57
1 rear panel	£70
1 rear inner lower panel	£45
Body mounting kit	£20

ENGINE MACHINING & PARTS	(£1,054)
Rebore block	£36
Full engine balance	£75
Ream small ends	£30
Surface cylinder head	£20

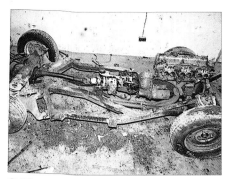

● *The central part of the chassis needed major repairs and the rest was renewed.*

● *Now the chassis is as sound and beautifully finished as the outer paintwork.*

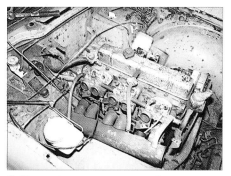

● *The engine compartment at the start - a dreadful mess and incomplete as well.*

including some very expensive models, indicated that price is no guide to reliability. The CSW11 semi-automatic spot welder (£223) proved entirely reliable and I am not surprised to discover that this one is widely used by professional restorers.

The Clarke (King 25) plasma cutter is a remarkably effective tool but at £457 it is quite expensive for a DIY restorer.

We used two compressors, an Airmaster Tiger 10/60 (£351, rated at 9cfm with a 50 litre tank) and an Airmaster AM 15EF150 (£470, rated at 14 cfm with a 150 litre tank). The latter is the equivalent of many a compressor that you will find permanently installed in a professional workshop but with an even larger tank. The Tiger 10/60 performed better than expected when we were painting the TR6 and this is a popular compressor.

The next larger belt-driven compressor is the Tiger 15/60 (£410, 14cfm) but there is a 14cfm economy model in between, the Tiger 15/55 costing £363, which features direct drive. Apparently belt-drive is considered the superior arrangement but perhaps the 15/55 would be worth considering when full-time everyday use is not anticipated. My own personal preference is the Tiger 15/60 and I should include a reminder here that displacement is not what matters. It is the free air delivery (fad) that matters and this is usually around 30% less than the cfm.

We didn't make any startling discoveries about the DeVilbiss JGA 30EX (£153) and the Binks BBR (£106) sprayguns other than that they both worked quite happily with the Tiger 10/60. In theory this shouldn't have happened but we were spraying individual wings, with pauses in between, rather than the whole bodyshell at one go. These are highly regarded professional guns for which spare parts and a wide range of alternative parts are readily available to suit different paint applications.

Common sense dictated that the Clarke Air Super Pro, at just under £40, shouldn't really be compared with the others, yet it performed very well indeed. In short, it does what it does very well but I would not expect it to be as versatile as the others (in terms of its adapability to various types of paint). Spare parts are available for the Clarke gun.

At just over £700, including VAT, I wouldn't expect many DIY restorers to be interested in the top-of-the-range engine crane which S.W. obtained from Machine Mart. However, a one-ton economy folding crane (£210) was added to Machine Mart's stock, too late for this project, but I understand that it is a very satisfactory crane and of course it can be transported easily and stored between use in very little space - just the sort of tool that could be shared between two or three owners. The same comment applies to the Dolly Trolleys (£117 each for the 6in model), of which two would be needed to support (say) a bare bodyshell, enabling it to be moved around

Breakdown of costs

Beadblast and surface flywheel	£25	Caliper pistons/pads/kits	£53	Interior side panels	£120
Cut valve seats/surface six valves	£21	Brake shoes	£15	Boot board, carpet and trim kit	£53
New crankshaft	£86	Rear wheel cylinders & kits	£36	Radiator cowling kit	£11
1 set pistons	£170	Handbrake cables	£14	Gearbox tunnel cover	£28
Big end/main bearings/thrusts/ seals	£43	Set brake hoses	£30	Centre console knee pads	£20
Camshaft	£80	Brake tubing (Kunifer) and fittings	£35	Dashboard	£160
1 set cam followers	£34	Brake master cylinder	£80	Dash top trim	£29
Rocker shaft	£30	Silicone brake fluid	£16	Dash left and right crash pad	£56
12 phosphor bronze bushed rockers	£114			Locks, handles,	
Oil pump	£35	**ELECTRICAL, LIGHTING ETC**	**(£975)**	pulls, links and mirror	£108
Head gasket set	£26			Recovering front seats	£280
Conversion gasket set	£13	Wiring loom (inc overdrive)	£180	Inertia seatbelts	£50
Set small end bushes	£12	1 pr front sidelights and indicators	£180	Set of sunvisors	£36
Clutch complete	£95	1 pr headlamp bowls, gaskets etc	£30	B-post cappings	£6
Valves (6 new), valve guides		Halogen headlamp kit	£20	GRP handbrake cable cover	£20
(inc. fitting) and springs	£74	Front wing side repeaters	£33	Motolita steering wheel	£105
Timing chain & tensioner, core plugs		Rear lamp lenses	£158	Speedo. (s'hand)	£50
& engine mounts	£35	Fuse box	£23	6 rear light bulb holders	£31
		Washer bottle and original motor	£45	Grille assembly	£75
GEARBOX & DIFF:		1 pr horns	£12	Grille lower trim panel	£16
		Number plate lamp and chrome cover	£65	2 headlamp rings	£23
Parts to rebuild original units	£316	Battery	£55	Front bumper (rechromed original)	£220
		Alternator	£35	Rear bumper complete	
STEERING, SUSPENSION & BRAKES	**(£1,134)**	2 Relays	£20	(rechromed original)	£146
		Switches, leads, plugs, coil etc	£119	Badges, transfers, wheel centres	£62
Steering rack mounts and lock stops	£10			Fuel filler cap	£20
2 top ball joints	£22	**FUEL INJECTION**	**(£504)**	Rubber seals and glass	£257
2 track rod ends	£10			Cooling and heating systems,	
2 trunnions	£36	Recon. fuel pump	£125	exhaust and hoses	£320
2 vertical links	£76	Pressure relief valve	£29	Shotblasting chassis,	
Trunnion/wishbone/anti-roll bar bushes etc	£41	Recon. metering unit	£110	body sections and suspension parts	£150
Front & rear link arms	£46	6 injectors	£96	Paint materials, fillers, stoppers etc	£525
2 front dampers	£34	Braid injection line set	£110	Cables, oils, filters and misc.	£338
All road springs	£71	Fuel piping, fittings & filter	£34		
4 trailing arm bushes	£20			**TOTAL ALL PARTS**	**£10,690**
5 tyres	£350				
1 set diff mounts & washers	£34	**TRIM, EXTERIOR CHROME ETC**	**(£2,430)**	**LABOUR:**	**£18,617**
6 U/Js	£30				
1 set rear shaft gaiters	£18	Hood (Everflex) made to measure	£250	1,379 hours at £13.50 per hour	
4 rear bump stops	£12	New hood frame	£175		
2 brake discs	£45	Rear hood to deck rail	£20	**TOTAL PLUS VAT AND MOT FEE.**	**£34,455**
		Carpets, made to measure	£260		

TR6 RESTORATION

● *The transformation - a few thousand pounds later at the fitting-up stage.*

● *Sports cars rarely have much luggage space, but the TR6 is better than some.*

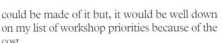

● *The superbly-finished dashboard. Yes, the engine was running when this shot was taken - note the position of the various needles!*

easily so that it was not a fixed obstacle in the workshop.

Blasting cabinets are not new on the DIY market and Machine Mart have a floor-standing unit (£699) and also a benchtop version (£581) with a slightly shallower chamber. You need a compressor (such as the Tiger 15/60) and a suitable vacuum cleaner to act as a dust extractor, making this very useful and effective facility somewhat expensive overall. Ideally the blasting facilities should be housed away from the mechanical workshop and the painting area, especially in professional workshops where all types of work are carried out simultaneously. I would certainly invest in a blasting cabinet eventually if I felt that plenty of use

could be made of it but, it would be well down on my list of workshop priorities because of the cost.

I must admit that I have changed my mind about parts washers since using the Machine Mart unit. Here again there is the free-standing unit which we used, the Clarke CW1 Parts Washer at £129, and a much smaller benchtop unit at £59. Both employ an electric pump to recirculate the cleaning fluid via a flexible hose which can be directed on to the work in hand. I used to think that it was a lot of money to pay for what is, in effect, a metal box with a lid, albeit with a built-in pump.

Since then I have become convinced that struggling along with a bucket of cleaning fluid

and a old paintbrush is a mug's game if it can be avoided and that anything which actually makes the task of cleaning filthy components quite pleasant is a good thing. Thus I have bought a CW1 Parts Washer for my own workshop, together with another very useful tool - a six-inch bench grinder with a stone at one end and a wire wheel at the other (£47). Incidentally, I neither asked nor received any favours from Machine Mart, just in case you are wondering but I am sure I don't know why I deprived myself of these tools for so long. Need I say more?

If you have mains electricity in your workshop but need an effective heater, the propane-burning Clarke Little Devil (£153) should be adequate for most workshops up to about 6,500 cubic feet and this is the smallest of Machine Mart's range of space heaters.

The other tools which we obtained from Machine Mart included Desoutter's Slimline Air Drill Model 106 and the 367 Sander, the Black and Decker P5411K angle grinder and sundry other items such as welding clamps and the 33lb anvil. None of these require any particular comment. In other words, they all proved reliable over a long period of daily use and if you want to avoid the hassle of selecting alternatives from the almost bewildering assortment of tools which are available from Machine Mart and elsewhere, you will not go far wrong if you settle for one of these.

All that remains is for me to thank our sponsors, Machine Mart, and this includes Nic Keeley whose help and advice throughout the project proved invaluable, and of course S.W. Classics who have now produced two superb restorations in a row for *Practical Classics*.

The companies who have been involved in this TR6 project are:
S. W. Classics, Brook House, Dartington, Nr Totnes, Devon. Tel: (0803) 865842.
Machine Mart Limited, 211 Lower Parliament Street, Nottingham NGI 1GN. Tel: (0602) 587666.
Autotrim, Filham Moor Industrial Estate, Ivybridge, Devon. Tel: 0752 893368.
Abbot Blasting of Newton Abbot, Bradley Lane, Newton Abbot. Tel: 0626 68684.
Cox and Buckles Spares, 22-28 Manor Road, Richmond, Surrey, TW9 1YB. Tel: 081 948 6666.
GEM Developments, Beacon Park, Plymouth. Tel: 0752 705989.
J and B. T. Engineering, Unit 3 Brook House, Dartington, Totnes, Devon TQ9 6DJ.
Clive Manvers, Unit 1 Buttons Green Farm, Cockfield, Bury St Edmunds, Suffolk, IP30 OJf. Tel: 0284 828674. Fax: 0284 827063.
Revington TR Spares, Home Farm, Middlezoy, Bridgwater, Somerset, TA7 0PD. Tel: 0823 69437. Fax: 698109.
Rimmer Bros Ltd, Triumph House, Sleaford Road, Bracebridge Heath, Lincoln, LN4 2NA. Tel. 0522 568000, Fax. 0522 567600.
TR Bitz, Lyncastle Way, Barley Castle Trading Estate, Appleton, Warrington, Cheshire, WA4 45T. Tel. 0925 861861, Fax. 0925 860816.
TR GB, 3 Warners Drove, Somersham, Huntingdon, Cambridgeshire PE17 3HW. Tel: 0487 842168. Fax: 740274.